China's Restructuring in Finance and Real Estate

5-7, rue de l’Ecole-Polytechnique, 75005 Paris

www.editions-harmattan.fr

ISBN : 978-2-343-17064-0
EAN : 9782343170640

ZHAO Yongsheng

China's Restructuring in Finance and Real Estate

L'Harmattan

Author: ZHAO Yongsheng, Prof./Dr. in the Economics and Finance, University of International Business and Economics (UIBE); Vice-President of the Paris-based Association des Juristes et des Economistes France-Chine.

This research has been supported by State Project No. 16ZDA141, "Historical Experience from the European Social Welfare System and its Inspirations for China".

The author sincerely thanks Professor Jean-Claude BERTHELEMY of Université Paris 1-Panthéon-Sorbonne, and Mrs. SONG Shengxia of Global Times for their assistance.

INTRODUCTION

Finance and real estate that this book aims to analyze are two significant variables for the economic growth of an emerging economy like China during its four decades' reform and opening-up.

Chapter One will analyze China's restructuring in finance: banking system reforms, credit system reforms, and the Chinese government's efforts to adopt the WTO-oriented reforms, including opening the banking and financial sector to foreign competition, and the restructuring of non-performing loans or assets—a thorny issue for Chinese State-owned banks and enterprises.

Chapter Two will focus on China's restructuring in real estate. After reviewing the complicated real estate reform from an old system to a new mechanism, the urban redevelopment as a special housing reform will be analyzed. Real estate in China is a controversial sector, which is a pillar of growth but faces a risky bubble. In fact, different economic and financial variables have contributed to the expansion of the Chinese housing market.

Finally, policy recommendations will be advanced.

CHAPTER 1

Financial Institutions' Restructuring

Western people consider China a labyrinth, and its financial system is even more of a labyrinth due to the Chinese system's opacity and complexity. In this section, I hope to provide clarity to that complexity.

SECTION 1 BANKING SYSTEM RESTRUCTURING

1. Banking System Before Reform

The PBOC, as "the center of cash, credit and settlement", delivered cash and granted credit. The cash held by urban residents and SOEs were to be deposited to the PBOC, and the settlement among different public sectors should also be made through the PBOC.

Although specialized banks had been founded under the PBOC like the Agricultural Bank of China (ABC), the Bank of China (BOC) and China Construction Bank (CCB), they were not independent. The PBOC has a virtually monopoly of banking activities in China, and these specialized banks exist only as a "department" of the PBOC or the Ministry of Finance.

It is not difficult for us to see that during the 30 years since the PRC was established to the start of the reform, from 1949-1978, China's banking system had undergone changes in terms of institutional setting. However, the all-in-one banking system had not been fundamentally changed by the reform and opening-up.

The banking system's main mission was to provide turnover capital (liquid funds) to enterprises. Consistent with the aforementioned situation, national savings at that time came mainly from the government. In 1978, government savings made up 15.5% of the GNP while accumulated residential savings only accounted for 6%. Moreover, the former was much more important than the latter. For the most part between 1962 and 1978, there was a slight surplus in government expenses minus disbursement for investment based on budget, and between 1958 and 1978, the Chinese government had neither internal nor external debt.

Before the reform and opening-up, the function of financial intermediation was limited in resource allocation as most investments were directly disbursed by the government instead of by the banking system. This limited banking activity was monopolized by the all-in-one banking system led by the PBOC. The result was the absence of a financial market, and almost no other financial assets other than banking savings.

2. Banking System At The Beginning of Reform

By the end of 1991, the PBOC had, aside from its headquarters in Beijing, 44 first-level branches in provinces and big cities, more than 400 second-level branches (between province and county) and about 2,000 subsidiary institutions at the county level. At that time, the PBOC had more than 166,000 employees.

As a central bank, the PBOC was a government administrative institution under the direct guidance of the State Council. Its main missions are to establish macro monetary policies, control monetary supply, regulate interest and exchange rates, exert the "cashbox" influence of the central government, regulate financial market and formulate comprehensive credit plans.

As an official representative of China, the PBOC has represented the government in international organizations such as the International Monetary Fund (IMF) since 1980 and Asian Development Bank (ADB) since 1985. In addition, the PBOC established under its guidance the State Administration of Foreign Exchange (SAFE) which is a government institution specializing in foreign currency control and management.

Aside from the PBOC, the Chinese banking system is composed of specialized banks and commercial banks. China has 4 State-owned specialized banks—the Industrial and Commercial Bank of China (ICBC), which initially specialized in lending to the industrial sector, the Agricultural Bank of China (ABC) for agricultural lending and rural development, the China Construction Bank (CCB) to develop large-scale and long-term infrastructure projects, and the Bank of China (BOC) for foreign exchange activities and to finance imports and exports.

The Rural Credit Cooperatives (RCCs) were the rural financial institutions which belong to the ABC and under its guidance. Tightly linked to the CCB, the China Investment Bank's (CIB) primary function is to arrange international financing mainly from the World Bank. China created several comprehensive commercial banks, including national banks like the Bank of Communications (BOCOM) and Citic Industrial Bank (CITICIB), and regional banks like Shenzhen Merchant Bank, Fujian Industrial Bank, Guangdong Development Bank and Shanghai Pudong Bank.

During the reform period, specialized banks were restructured and new commercial banks and financial institutions were also set up. The primary mission of specialized banks is to run commercial banking activities in its specific fields. At the same time, they are required to provide policy-directed credit and to implement economic policies based on government instructions. Here is a brief discussion on China's major banks and financial institutions.

Seven Banks

The Industrial and Commercial Bank of China (ICBC) was established on January 1, 1984 simultaneously with the PBOC. Its primary mission is to take over the commercial bank of the PBOC so that the latter can operate as a central bank. The ICBC collects savings from different sources and provides commercial banking services to urban residents, enterprises and other working units. The ICBC is the predominant source of State-owned and collectivity-owned enterprises' loans as turnover capital, to settle transactions of enterprises and other working units, and to supervise the firms' financial activities.

The Agricultural Bank of China (ABC) was established in 1955 primarily to provide financial services to rural residents and other working units. The ABC is the government's main channel for loans to rural regions. It also guides and supervises transactions for rural credit cooperatives (RCCs).

Founded in 1954, the China Construction Bank (CCB) provides large-scale capital formation and funds for reconstruction projects. The CCB is also under the Ministry of Finance. Since 1985, all infrastructure disbursements turned into loans, which made it more of a real bank than an institution of the Ministry of Finance.

The Bank of China (BOC) oversees foreign exchange transactions and international balances. It is not only a place to settle trade and related international activities but also an import-export bank which grants loans related to international trade. The BOC manages foreign exchange, provides international loans and supervises foreign securities activity. However, since the reform, its monopoly status in international financial activities was challenged by the other new financial institutions.

The China Investment Bank (CIB) was established in December 1981 and specializes in providing medium- and long-term foreign credit in China, most of which focuses on small and medium projects. The CIB works closely with the World Bank, Asian Development Bank and other international monetary institutions, and serves as the intermediary of loans under the guidance of credit institutions.

Restructured in July 1986, BOCOM has two unique functions: First, most of its shares are owned by the central government, and second, unlike other specialized banks with strict business restrictions, BOCOM is engaged in a wide variety of financial activities.

Owned by local cooperatives, RCCs are an independent credit consortium in rural regions, and serve as grass-root agricultural banks. The RCCs are relatively small in scale and can make their own decisions and are accountable to them.

"Bogaidai" **(From Disbursement To Loan)**

During the reform, efforts were made with respect to Bogaidai (change from budgetary disbursement to banking loans). The financial link between enterprises and government finance departments was gradually severed. In 1979, enterprises were allowed to partially retain profits. "A tax instead of profit delivery" (Ligaishui) reform followed from 1983 to 1985 (which was partly rescinded by the enterprise contract responsibility system from 1988-1992). The task of providing working capital and new investment funds shifted to the banking system in an effort to switch from budget appropriations to credit (Bogaidai). (Anne-Laure Delatte, Julien Fouquau and Carsten A. Holz, "Explaining Money Demand in China during the Transition from a Centrally Planned to a Market-based Monetary System", BOFIT Discussion Papers 27/2011, October 2011)

The proportion of investments by disbursement rapidly decreased, and to enhance efficiency and visualize capital costs, the use of banking loans was expanded to include fixed capital investments. More and more fixed capital, including large-scale key projects, was financed by banking loans instead of budgetary disbursements.

Thus, the banking system was becoming more important. On one hand, as residential savings quickly grew and became the economy's largest source of savings, the banking system had become the major financial intermediary to channel savings to investments; on the other hand, the banking system not only supplied a large part of turnover funds but also supplied fixed capital loans. Hence, bank loans were becoming extremely important in maintaining the economy and in controlling State macro credit.

3. Banking Reform During Last Decade

During the last decade, China's banking system launched a series of reform measures and a relatively complete and open banking system was gradually emerging.

1) Establishing Policy Banks

"Policy banks" refer to financial institutions established, participated in or guaranteed by the government and focused on carrying out or acting in accordance with the government's economic policies instead of seeking profit. They engage, directly or indirectly, in policy financing activities in specific business areas and play the role of financial institutions in the place of government in promoting economic growth, stimulate social progress and manage the macro economy.

According to the Decision of the State Council on Reform of the Financial System and other documents determined by the Communist Party of China (CPC), the government established three "policy" banks: the China Development Bank (CDB), the Agricultural Development Bank of China (ADBC) and the Export-Import Bank of China (EXIMBC) in 1994.

These banks have four functions:

— To assist commercial banks in developing the specific sectors which these banks do not economically appreciate without support from the government;

— To orient the funds from other fields to invest in the specific sectors so as to generate the "effect of multiplication", and to nurse and manage these sectors before pushing them into the market;

— To supervise the use of funds in implementing closed-off management to ensure the optimization of policy funds;

— To allow the State, through the intervention of policy banks, to regulate so as to ensure a balanced development of specific sectors and other sectors.

The differences between policy banks and specialized banks are as follows:

The three policy banks were established in 1994 to take over the government-directed spending functions of the four State-owned commercial banks (Big Four). The ADBC provides funds for agricultural development projects in rural areas, the CDB specializes in infrastructure financing, and the EXIMBC specializes in trade financing. Policy banks are therefore responsible for financing economic and trade development and State-invested projects.

The specialized banks are the banks operating in specific fields and offering specific financial services, whose emergence is actually required for the financial sector to adapt to the development of diversification and China's economic growth.

The policy banks were born out of the specialized banks in 1994. The so-called "policy" businesses were peeled from specialized banks and these "policy" businesses would be operated by the newly created policy banks. This was done to transform the banking sector (commercialization) in China, and the financial reform in 1994 separated policy finance from commercial finance.

2) Promulgate Two Laws

The Law on the PBOC of the PRC was approved by the National People's Congress (NPC) on March 18, 1995 and revised on December 27, 2003, also by the NPC. The Law on Commercial Banks of the PRC was approved by the NPC on May 10, 1995 and revised on December 27, 2003. These two laws were quasi concomitant. Since the promulgation of these two laws, China's banking system followed a more legal path.

3) Branches By Economic Regions

In 1998, the PBOC started setting up branches according to the economic regional classification and by the start of 1999, nine trans-provincial branches and two business management departments (Beijing and Chongqing) had been successively established.

In light of the reform's blueprint, the primary mission of these branches was to implement national monetary policy and to supervise financial activities, except securities and insurance, within the areas under the administration. For the provincial capitals and the cities specifically designated in the State plan where branches had not been set up, financial supervision offices were established as the branches' agencies.

4) State-Owned AMCs (Asset Management Companies)

In 1999, to reduce the bad assets of State-owned commercial banks, the government founded four asset management companies (AMCs)—China Cinda Asset Management Co.,Ltd., China Huarong Asset Management Co.,Ltd., China Orient Asset Management Co.,Ltd. and China Great Wall Asset Management Co.,Ltd. These AMCs bought at book price 1.4 trillion RMB of bad assets from the four banks (CCB, ICBc, BOC and ABC), including 405 billion RMB worth of shares transferred from the debt of 601 SOEs.

There were three channels to finance this acquisition: 40 billion RMB as the basic fund from the State budget to these four AMCs, 570 billion RMB for re-lending supplied by the PBOC, and 820 billion RMB in financial securities issued by the four AMCs towards their respective banks.

The AMCs are State-owned financial institutions of sole proprietorship and as independent legal entities. Each of them has the same registered capital of 10 billion RMB disbursed directly by the Ministry of Finance. The AMCs' major mission and operation targets are to acquire, manage and treat the bad assets peeled from the four big banks and to save the assets to reduce losses and address financial risks.

The AMCs will be analyzed in detail in the forthcoming section, "Treatment of Non-Performing Loans (NPLs)".

5) Establishment of the CBRC

Based on the Decision on the Plan for Restructuring the State Council made by the First Session of the 11th NPC, the State Council established the China Banking Regulatory Commission (CBRC). The CBRC assumed its functions on April 28, 2003 and supervises the banking sector, AMCs, trust and investment companies (TICs) and other financial institutions to maintain the legal and robust operation of the banking sector.

6) Shanghai Headquarters

Shanghai is China's economic capital and one of engines of the country's economic growth, especially financial growth. The Shanghai headquarters of the PBOC was established on August 10, 2005 in response to the needs of China's expanding banking system, to ameliorate the central bank system, to more effectively play the role of the central bank as the economy's macro regulator, and also accelerate the Shanghai's development as an international financial center, which the Chinese government expects to overtake Hong Kong and Tokyo.

PBOC's Shanghai headquarters is based on the structure of the bank's Shanghai branch, and operates as an integral component of the branch under the latter's direction and authorization. Its major missions are to assume the central bank's role and certain management responsibilities.

The WTO-oriented banking reforms were launched in 2002 after China's accession to the WTO in November 2001. This theme will be analyzed in Section 3, WTO-Oriented Reforms, Chapter 1.

To date, China's banking system has been developed into a complete system under the PBOC's direction, with the State-owned commercial banks as the main body complemented by policy banks, other commercial banks and foreign and joint venture banks.

4. Rural Credit Cooperatives (RCCs)

Non-banking sector reform is also a theme which cannot be ignored in China. We will focus on one representative example—the Rural Credit Cooperatives (RCCs).

RCCs were founded in 1951, two years after the PRC's birth, and their numbers reached 103,000 by 1957. The RCCs had become an important financial institution for agricultural production at that time.

After this preliminary stage, the RCCs regressed not only in quantity but also in quality from 1958 to 1978 due to the negative impact of social and cultural movements. In the preliminary stage, the RCCs were managed by the PBOC and organized on the basis of the credit cooperatives criteria. But during the two decades they were managed by people's communes and production brigades, and none of the cooperative standards were respected.

When the reform and opening-up began, the RCCs' management was transferred to the Agricultural Bank of China from 1980 to 1996, and had become a basic institution of the ABC. By the end of 1996, the RCCs were separated from ABC, and the PBOC began to take over their management and supervision.

Since 2003 the RCCs were placed under the supervision of the China Banking Regulatory Commission (CBRC). In March 2003, the first agricultural cooperative bank in China was established in Yinzhou Village, Ningbo, Zhejiang Province. This was a breakthrough in the history of rural financial system reform in China.

In the case of the Yinzhou Agricultural Cooperative Bank (YACB), the minimum amount needed to buy a share was only 1,000 RMB (125 Euros, 1 Euro=8 RMB). That led a rapid rise in the number of shareholders to over 10,000. The YACB not only accepted shares from ordinary people but from legal personalities as well.

The equity capital of the YACB is divided into two categories: The first is called qualification stock and the other is investment stock. The former can enjoy preferential services from the bank, and can be withdrawn after three years, while shareholders of the latter cannot withdraw but can transfer their shares.

With numerous reforms, the YACB was provided with a modern financial system, with its equity capital quickly rising to 220.1 million RMB (27.51 million Euro). The performance was encouraging: it accounted for over 33% of the market in terms of savings and over 40% in loans. Its performance surpassed most commercial banks or financial institutions.

After Yinzhou, the rest of China followed. We will cite cases in two provinces—Jiangxi and Anhui.

From 2004 to 2014, the total amount of savings and loans of the RCCs in Jiangxi Province had decoupled within a decade. In 2014, the balance of all savings categories was over 430 billion RMB (53.75 billion Euro), representing 21% of the banking sector and the highest in Jiangxi, and the balance of all loan categories exceeded 260 billion RMB (32.50 billion Euro), or 18% of the banking sector in Jiangxi.

In Anhui Province, local financial institutions had the biggest share of savings and loans as well as the most sub-branches and the largest network. The ratio of NPLs had decreased from 39.9% to 2.24% from the eve of the reform and opening-up to June 2014.

SECTION 2 CREDIT SYSTEM RESTRUCTURING

We will go into detail on the evolution of China's credit system to help demystify China's finance growth nexus. The modern Chinese credit system has its origins in the planned credit system established just after the People's Republic of China was established. The credit reform gradually converted the planned credit system to a market-based one, and the credit functions were also transformed from administrative monetary distribution to resource allocation and a financing function.

1. Establishment Of The Planned Credit System

Pre-Reform: Nationalization and Financial Monopoly

China was obliged to choose a strategy which prioritized the development of the heavy industry at the start of the PRC based on the specific international and domestic political and economic environment. Nevertheless, the heavy industry required huge investments and took time to develop, while the PRC lacked funds and production costs were initially too high for China's new government if the purchases were made at market prices.

Together with the process of nationalization, China built its monopolistic financial structure. Even today, when we try to analyze that period's credit system, we realize that this is the direct result of national development strategies of that era, and that the nationalization and financial monopoly were the only choice that the Chinese government could make to ensure financing for the essential huge projects the government considered as "pivot projects".

Nationalization ensured that the banking efficiency was consistent with the general national efficiency, and the monopoly ensured that savings was mobilized by the country for the country. The financial arrangements through the national monopoly ensured maximum savings mobilization and a credit allocation in line with the country's needs.

China realized the need for the nationalization of banks and the financial system with the PBOC as the hub of China's banking system. At that time, the PBOC was the only representative of China's financial property rights.

Credit Planned allocation

The Chinese government chose to use credit planned allocation in the first stage of the PRC to finance the operations of SOEs through the national financial monopoly at low interest rates.

After China established the State monopolistic financial ownership, to ensure the national priority of heavy industrialization was properly executed, the PBOC in 1953 created the credit management institutions in its subsidiary banks to implement the comprehensive credit plans. China developed a credit management system called "Tongshoutongzhi", that is, subsidiary banks had to submit to the headquarters of banks all savings collected, and credit was also to be allocated in a unified and step-ladder manner based on the planned quotas checked and set by their headquarters (Lin Yifu et al., 1994).

The planned credit system was the endogenous product of the planned economic system in China, and this sort of credit system matched well with the State ownership-based economic system. However, when the initial stage of industrialization had been realized and the basic economic structure established, the planned credit system could not work any more.

2. Credit and Taxes

The real economy was separated from the virtual economy under the State-owned planned economy. The economy planning included the physical flow and planning based on the monetary flow. Since its creation in 1953, the former State Planning Commission adopted the unified allocation system for important resources.

The allocation of resources under China's planned economy was accomplished on the basis of physical balance and through the physical distribution by the State. Hence, the currency played a "shadow" role of the physical distribution in the economy. The currency's role was passive and that of finance was also an accessory just like tools in a limited confine during the process of resource distribution planned and manipulated by the government. As most materials adopted the physical distribution mode, the monetary flow continued to play a subordinate role, which demonstrated the planned economy in the form of currency without any initiative or function of orienting resource allocation.

There were two channels for the State to concentrate monetary resources: One was through fiscal and financial channels, and the other through the banks. As previously mentioned, China developed a credit management system called "Tongshoutongzhi". The same method was used in Chinese SOEs, and China established "Tongshoutongzhi" vis-a-vis SOEs.

In the "Tongshoutongzhi" system, all the the SOE's profits and depreciated funds should be submitted to the State and channeled into the arrangements of the State's budget, while the State would disburse the necessary funds to all SOEs to satisfy their financial needs, including funds for infrastructure construction, renewal of fixed assets, technical transformation, the new products' trial manufacturing, and the purchase of other dispersed fixed assets. The liquidity needed for the enterprises' production would also be disbursed by the State's financial department (Lin Yifu et al., 1994).

SOEs' revenue mainly consisted of profit and depreciated funds, and accounted for over 40% of the State's fiscal revenue since 1954, and over 50% during the years preceding the reform and opening-up, and reached 63.9% in 1960. The following table reflects the evolution of China's financial structure from 1950-1978.

Table 1: Structure of Government Revenue and Expenditures in China 1950-1978 (Unit: 100 million RMB, %)

Year	Structure of Fiscal Revenues		Structure of Financial Expenditures				Basic Construction Fee minus Enterprises' Revenue
	Enter-prises' Reve-nue	Enterprises' Revenue/ Total Fiscal Revenues	Economic Constru-ction Fee	Economic Construction Fee/Total Financial Expenditures	Basic Constru-ction Expendi-tures/ Economic Constru-ction Fee	Added Disburse-ment for Enter-prises' Liquidity/ Economic Constru-ction Fee	
1950	8.7	14.0	17.4	25.5	72.0	0.0	8.7
1951	30.5	24.4	35.1	28.8	77.0	0.0	4.6
1952	57.3	32.9	73.2	42.6	63.7	25.3	16.0
1953	76.7	36.0	87.4	39.9	80.5	15.8	10.7
1954	99.6	40.6	123.6	50.6	68.2	21.3	24.0
1955	111.9	44.9	137.6	52.4	64.3	22.4	25.7
1956	134.3	47.9	159.1	53.3	87.7	6.8	24.9
1957	144.2	47.6	163.0	55.1	75.9	12.8	18.9
1958	189.2	49.8	278.9	69.7	82.3	9.2	89.7
1959	279.1	57.3	389.3	71.7	77.7	13.9	110.2
1960	365.8	63.9	460.7	71.6	76.9	14.6	94.9
1961	191.3	53.7	210.0	59.0	52.5	14.0	18.7
1962	146.2	46.6	152.6	51.8	36.5	31.3	6.4
1963	172.7	50.5	174.1	52.4	46.1	21.0	1.4
1964	212.9	53.3	210.0	53.3	59.0	11.1	-2.9
1965	264.3	55.8	254.1	55.2	62.4	10.8	-10.2
1966	333.3	59.7	309.4	57.6	61.7	13.0	-23.9
1967	218.5	52.1	244.0	55.5	66.1	11.9	25.6

1968	166.7	46.2	166.0	46.4	71.0	7.2	-0.7
1969	286.7	54.4	295.5	56.2	69.8	9.0	8.8
1970	379.0	57.2	392.6	60.5	76.0	8.0	13.6
1971	428.4	57.5	418.3	57.1	74.0	8.4	-10.1
1972	445.7	58.1	432.0	56.4	71.6	9.9	-13.7
1973	457.0	56.4	468.3	57.9	67.7	11.5	11.3
1974	407.3	52.0	460.9	58.3	67.9	9.7	53.7
1975	400.2	49.1	481.7	58.7	67.9	8.7	81.5
1976	338.1	43.5	466.2	57.8	66.8	9.7	128.2
1977	402.4	46.0	493.7	58.5	60.9	13.3	91.4
1978	572.0	50.5	719.0	64.1	62.9	9.3	147.0

Source: Ministry of Finance of People's Republic of China, (Dong, 2009)

The "Tongshoutongzhi" financial system and the labor distribution system based on low salaries would engender the savings structure with specific Chinese characteristics before the reform and opening-up. Most of the savings was in the form of government savings, while the savings of enterprises and residents were both miniscule.

This kind of savings structure justified the innate comparative advantages of taxes in the collection of monetary resources. Also called pecuniary resources, monetary resources are assets in the form of money.

In 1953, the savings balance including urban and rural areas reached 1.23 billion RMB, which represented only 5.8% of total fiscal revenues. The fiscal revenues are the revenues of or related to government finances, especially tax revenues. In the following quarter of a century, this ratio, Savings Balance/Fiscal Revenues, was maintained at less than 20% except in rare cases.

Figure 1: Fiscal Revenues and Savings Balance in the Urban-Rural Areas

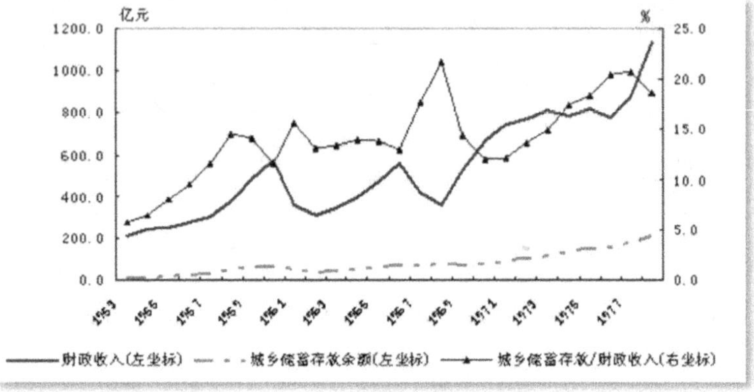

Fiscal Revenues (L) Total Saving Balance (L) Balance/Fiscal Revenues (R). Source: Almanac of China's Finance and Banking, 1998, Ministry of Finance of People's Republic of China

Since the majority of resources were under the control of the National Finance, which is similar to the UK's Public Finance, finance naturally became the main channel for SOE funds. After collecting fiscal revenues, the State would allocate more than half of it (could reach as high as 70%) to the SOEs based on the national budget planning and through investments and liquidity disbursements, and most of the investments (usually between 60% and 80%) were focused on huge infrastructure projects.

With most of the monetary resources controlled not only during the collection process but also during the allocation process, the National Finance played a vital role above SOBs, which only played a subordinate role. This is one of the unique characteristics of China's banking system, and this survives to this day despite profound reforms to the banking system.

Because of their subordinate role, banks only provided a miniscule amount of credit. Banks at that time were a "device", and merely monitored the costs of China's industrialization process. That's why banks were placed under the Ministry of Finance, and this lasted from 1969 to 1978.

The State tried to increase the weight of bank transfers through a tight restriction over cash transactions to bring into play the SOBs' monitoring function over the enterprises' revenues and expenditures.

The SOBs' credit function was limited to loans for temporary and seasonal liquidity requirements. That's why we still call this phenomenon during that period "Big Finance, Small banks".

3. Decentralization Reform

We have just analyzed the secondary role of credit in national monetary resource allocation under the planned credit system. We also know that this secondary role depended on the existence of a very strong National Finance.

After the launch of the reform and opening-up in 1978, people started to ask more questions about the situation of the National Finance, which faced growing problems after operating for many years under the planned economy.

The SOEs' fund requirements knew no limits while the National Finance faced increasing pressure to satisfy the financing needs of SOEs. At the same time, changes in the savings structure generated by the reforms gradually transformed the status of credit and the National Finance in the collection and allocation of monetary resources. The National Finance's role waned and that of credit rose. However, with the existence of the planned credit allocation system, credit could only complement the National Finance.

China's financial reforms were similar to other reforms in China, which centered around the decentralization of decision-making. The rapid development of the national economy and the progress of multiple reforms exposed two problems in the planned economy system due to the rise in the number and size of enterprises and the rapid increase in fabricated products.

There existed an information crisis. Chinese central planning authorities and the planned system were neither able to effectively monitor and control the entire national economy nor make sound decisions. The complexity of the relationship between supply and demand also created an information crisis. Planning authorities found it difficult planning for society's supply and demand because they did not have the market prices which reflected such supply and demand. These authorities found it difficult to maintain the equilibrium of society's material needs. Moreover, it was difficult for planners to deal with delegation and stimulation matters and the lack of efficiency in the micro operating mechanism caused a supply problem in the entire economy.

The "decentralization" economic reform was launched amid the aforementioned circumstances—first in the rural areas, then to the urban areas. The Chinese government adopted several measures. They first phased out the people's commune system (Renmin Gongshe Zhidu) and the agricultural cooperation system (Nongcun Hezuoshe Zhidu) in the rural areas, and established the household contract responsibility system (Jiating Lianchan Chengbao Zeren Zhidu) in its place. And the second measure focused on urban areas. Administrative procedures were simplified and the SOEs retained part of their profits.

The SOE reform broadened the enterprises' management autonomy, the State gradually reduced mandatory State planning in the SOEs' operations which allowed the SOEs greater authority over product pricing and sales, and the authority to determine salaries and bonuses.

To improve the relationship between the SOEs and the government, China launched in the mid-1980s two reforms called "Ligaishui" (Tax for Profit), which required SOEs to pay taxes instead of turning over their profits to the administration. The State Council introduced this reform in 1983 by imposing a 55 percent income tax on medium and large SOEs rather than taking their profits. Other measures soon followed, creating a complete tax scheme to encourage competition. This was one of the earliest steps taken to reform the SOEs and establish a national tax system, showing that a mature market might be an effective way to improve industrial efficiency (China Daily, August 2009).

Following these two reforms, the central government implemented another reform measure, "Lishuifenliu" (payment of tax plus a percentage of profits to the State) in 1988. Thanks to a series of reform measures, peasants, enterprises and workers enjoyed greater management autonomy and the right to choose, and profound changes took place in the revenue distribution system. This was the transformation from the "distribution according to work" system to the system with multiple distribution modes.

The direct result of the changes in distribution system was the change in the national income's distribution pattern, a rapid and continuous reduction in governmental income and a significant increase in personal income. Government revenue was reduced from 33.5% in 1978 to 12.4% in 1995, and the final distribution of the national income showed that government revenue was reduced from 31.6% in 1978 to 13.4% in 1995, while personal incomes increased from 50.5% to 69.1% for the same period.

Prior to the reforms, national fiscal revenue accounted for 25% of GDP and peaked at 40%. It was trimmed to 31.2% in 1978, the start of the reform and opening-up started. With the national financial capacity reduced, national fiscal revenues dropped to 10.7% of GDP in 1995. This downward trend was due to the individual-oriented income distribution system and changes in management.

Table 2: Final Distribution Pattern of National Income 1978-1995 (%)

Year	State's Reve - nue	Enter - prises' Revenue	Individual Revenue	Individual Revenue of Urban Areas	Individual Revenue of Rural Areas
1978	31.6	17.9	50.5	20.1	30.4
1979	27.2	19.2	53.6	20.5	33.1
1980	23.7	19.6	56.7	22.0	34.7
1981	21.7	17.9	60.4	21.8	38.6
1982	20.5	19.9	59.6	21.7	37.9
1983	20.6	19.2	60.2	21.3	38.9
1984	20.9	18.2	60.9	21.9	39.0
1985	20.9	17.7	61.4	23.4	38.0
1986	19.3	17.9	62.8	25.7	37.1
1987	16.9	19.4	63.7	26.8	36.9
1988	14.5	20.9	64.6	27.3	37.3
1989	14.4	21.5	64.1	27.9	36.2
1990	14.5	21.5	64.0	29.1	34.9
1991	13.7	20.9	64.4	30.6	33.8
1992	11.6	20.1	68.3	34.6	33.7
1993	11.5	20.7	67.8	36.7	31.1
1994	10.9	19.5	69.6	38.0	31.6
1995	13.4	17.5	69.1		

Source: State Planning Commission, "The Distribution Problems of China's Inhabitant Income" (Zhang, 1999)

4. Finance And Credit: Down And Up

The individual-oriented income distribution system had brought the direct change in the structure of national saving: Individual savings went up while the State's savings went down. The upward trend in individual savings meant that the monetary resources were distributed more evenly, and the SOBs were more efficient compared with the collection of taxes. It is easy to understand because as a free and compulsory system, tax collection had a relatively higher cost due to its dispersed monetary resources while the SOBs had a cost advantage.

In 1978, national fiscal revenues were 5.4 times higher than the savings balance in urban and rural areas; on the contrary, since 1986, the latter started to overtake the former, and in 2006 fiscal revenues were only 24% of the savings balance in urban and rural areas for the same period.

Figure 2: Comparison between Fiscal Revenues and Saving Balance in the Urban-Rural Areas 1978-2006

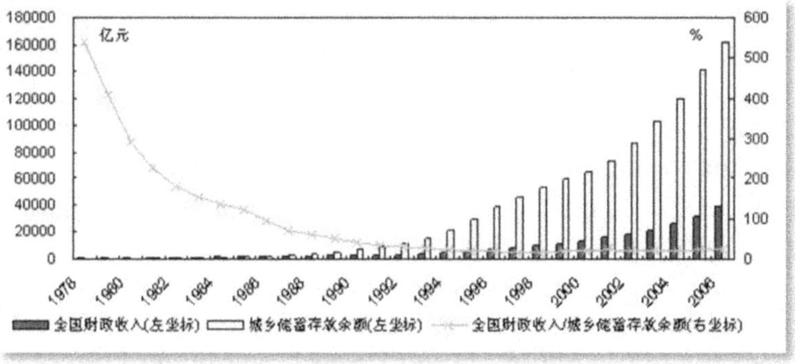

Fiscal Revenues (L) Total Saving Balance (L) Balance/Fiscal Revenues (R). Source: Ministry of Finance of People's Republic of China and People's Bank of China, (Dong, 2009)

The decline in the State's financial capacity has brought a drop in the Chinese government's capacity in funds as a nationwide investor. From 1978 to 1981, national expenditures for the infrastructure were reduced against conventional wisdom. It was 25.76 billion RMB in 1981 and gradually increased, but only slowly. Even as of 1995, expenditures reached only 78.92 billion RMB, almost the same amount for infrastructure as in 1958.

Liquidity from the State to SOEs also started to drop sharply starting 1978: It was only 960 million RMB in 1988, lower than any year before 1978. Fortunately, technology funds for renovation were not reduced, and even increased somewhat. That level rose 1.3 times from 1978-1988, and reached 22.36 billion RMB in 1992.

We can divide the Chinese enterprises in those years into two categories: One are the SOEs and the other are the non-SOEs. The decentralization reform focused on the SOEs, giving more power to these enterprises and to people working in the SOEs. Another reform was focused on the non-SOEs, also called "outside system enterprises" (Tizhiwai Qiye). The reform has settled the problem of stimulation in the SOEs, and encouraging the non-SOEs dealt with competition.

However, the decentralization reform only resolved one among a host of problems that constrained the SOEs during their development process. The stimulation measures that the SOEs only had a short-term effect without the capacity to create a sustainable stimulation system.

This void in the SOE reform would be supported by the non-SOEs reform, as the latter enjoyed a more flexible mechanism, could be more productive and competitiveness comparing with the SOEs. From 1985 to 1990, the competitiveness of the SOEs had increased by 23.6% while the collective enterprises from the town level increased by 73.8%, and that of other similar players, especially from the industrial sector of other types of ownership, increased by 82.2%. One-third of the SOEs were in the red due to their slow improvement in efficiency and the fall in competitiveness. The percentage of loss-incurring enterprises within the State budget was

31.0% and 29.7%, respectively, for 1990 and 1991 (Lin Yifu et al., 1994).

The heavy losses of the SOEs meant that maintaining these SOEs' operations would need more funding while the decline in the national financial capacity made it impossible for the State to provide sufficient funds to the SOEs. As previously mentioned, the SOBs had the advantage of saving, and this advantage helped SOBs tackle the SOEs financing dilemma. It was the intent of the State to shift the funding burden from the National Finance to the SOBs, and idem for the State-owned financial system which will replace the functions of the National Finance.

The SOBs supplied not only with virtually all the liquidity needed by the SOEs but also started to provide long-term funding. Obviously, in providing funds to the SOEs, the importance of the National Finance declined while that of credit increased significantly. The "Bogaidai" reform (change from budgetary disbursement to banking loans) was launched under these circumstances in 1985 vis-a-vis infrastructure investment within the State budget. This measure was made a transition for the National Finance in terms of long-term funding.

To adapt to the new situation, China started the transition from a highly centralized financial system to a professional State-owned banking system. In 1979, three banks were created—ABC, BOC and CCB—to support agricultural credit, foreign exchange and investment credit. ICBC was founded in 1984, whose purpose was to provide industrial and commercial enterprises liquidity loans and medium-term loans for investing in equipment. At the same time PBOC started to assume its central functions and would not be responsible for the businesses of commercial banks as before.

Two factors helped credit rapidly increase: One was the SOE operations dilemma and the other was the rapid development of non-SOE businesses. Even with the rapid increase in SOBs' savings, it still lagged largely behind the credit needs of the real economy during that period. Hence, China continued to adopt a planned credit system for relatively a long period after the reform due to contradictions between the supply and demand for loans granted by SOBs, and to ensure that the SOEs received funding. Of course, the planned credit system was not the same as before the reform, as the planned control began to open up.

With the increase in credit demand, the Chinese government, in its efforts to reform the Chinese credit fund management system from 1979-1994, was on how to reinforce the mobilization of savings and the appropriate credit autonomy of the SOBs. In April 1979, the State started to adopt a new management system called the "unified plan, management by grade, and link between deposits and loans".

Under this new management system, the PBOC made checks on the credit planning approved by the State based on all the annual balance plans between the revenues and the expenditures submitted by the branch banks in provinces, cities and regions. After the PBOC verified the balance between deposits and loans, city-level branches would manage local specialized banks.

It was the first time in the PRC's history to link the deposits with the loans, and this was significant in China's financial reform. From then on, deposits would justify the granting of loans. In February 1981, the balance method (deposits-loans) of control was modified, and a new method of lump balance was adopted. All specialized banks were able to operate within this method, checked and ratified by PBOC headquarters. That meant more deposits could justify more loans.

Principal banks started to focus on how to attract more deposits and increase the scale of loans. This became the banks' target. Admittedly, the development level of banks at this stage remained scale-oriented. But a major reform in credit management had been established.

This reform in 1985 was a crucial one in the credit management system because it paved the way for the formation of China's future credit market. Although strict credit planning still existed, credit had expanded. The inter-bank lending and borrowing was made possible and even within a bank, this sort of operations was permitted among subsidiary institutions, and specialized banks could apply for loans from a commercial bank. With these reform measures, the funds of specialized banks were not limited to savings any more.

The potential for credit expansion demonstrated the fund capacity for these specialized banks to the State, and did not mean the expansion of their operating autonomy. The State-owned specialized banks had to continue to provide credit to key projects, like national or SOE projects. The government asked these banks if it was necessary for them to distribute the so-called "welfare credit" to maintain social stability. In 1992, the policy credit of the four big SOBs accounted for 35.3% of their total credit business (IMF, 1994).

The direct result of non-market credit granted by these SOBs was to accumulate NPLs, and this increasingly threatened the State's financial security. Hence, the State looked to commercialize the specialized banks i.e. to reform the granting of credit from the distribution mode to the debit and credit mode based on market forces. But the high moral hazard generated by the massive policy loans threatened the survival of the commercialization of loans.

To prevent the moral hazard between policy and commercial credit, the Chinese government created in 1994 three policy banks for policy credit. Since then, SOBs started to follow market rules. The management of asset-debt ratio was introduced for the first time into the credit management system, and the level of debts (savings) was used to control the level of assets (credit). The SOBs' role as fund supplier for SOEs gradually weakened.

We have reviewed the establishment of the PRC's planned credit system from the nationalization and financial monopoly to the credit planned allocation. Then we discussed the relationship between credit and taxes, the decentralization launched with the start of the reform and opening-up, and finally finance and credit with a focus on the relationship between the National Finance and credit. After multiple reforms, the credit proceeded on the right track.

SECTION 3 WTO-ORIENTED RESTRUCTURING

1. WTO-Oriented Banking Restructuring

China officially joined the WTO on November 10, 2001. Trade ministers from across the world officially approved China's entry into the World Trade Organization (WTO) after 15 years of negotiations. The move was approved unanimously at the WTO's ministerial meeting in Qatar...and brings a market of 1.3 billion people into the global trading system.

What can the world expect from China? China's entry is expected to boost economic reforms started in the world's most populous nation more than 20 years ago and open its huge market to the rest of the world.

This is a real event in all fields for the "once-isolated communist China". (CNN, November 2001) It will be also a big stimulus for Chinese finance, especially for Chinese banking system reforms.

The year 2002 will, in my opinion, be an important watershed in the history of Chinese banking reforms. By adopting measures like injecting capital from the government, preferential fiscal policies, introducing foreign capital, and the IPO (initial public offering) in overseas markets, the financial situation had been largely ameliorated for major banks in China, and some banks had even started exploring new banking activities.

Under these circumstances and by respecting engagement with the WTO when China acceded to this organization, the Chinese government launched reforms on all restrictions in 2006 to completely open up the banking market. However, we are not aware o the actual conditions of Chinese commercial banks in terms of assets composition, profitability, diversity and corporate governance.

If China wants to ensure a sustainable and stable economic growth, further financial reform is necessary. The Chinese banking system reform will be the "avant garde" in Chinese finance considering its overwhelming position in China.

China's banking system reform has become an essential theme for the Chinese government in the marketization of its economy especially after China's accession to the WTO, and this theme includes further dealing with bad debts, an increase in fund distribution efficiency, enforcement of corporate governance and relaxing financial market restrictions and other measures.

1) Three Phases

Financial reforms in China can be summarized as a step-by-step marketization of financial system. We can divide Chinese financial reforms, including banking reforms, into three major phases:

Phase I: The period starting 1978 to 1992 can be defined as the start of the reform and opening-up. This phase broke the uni-banking system in China. Four independent SOCBs were set up, and the securities market and shareholder-based commercial banks were likewise created.

Phase II: This period lasted from 1993-1997. China separated policy banks and commercial banks, passed banking laws, bill laws and assurance laws, unified the inter-banking and foreign exchange markets, and deepened the concept of a socialist market economy.

Phase III: This the ongoing period which began during the 1997 Asian financial crisis. Although China began to alter State-owned Banks in 2002, one year after China's accession to the WTO, and that its financial reform had made tremendous changes in marketization and opening-up, reforms continue to this day. Despite that, opinions were split: One considers the situation stable, while the other says unstable factors prevail.

2) Circumstances On The Eve of WTO Accession

China's economy should be "internationalized". China had no other choice but to participate in the global economic "tide", and this was a perfect time to enter the WTO. What were the circumstances on the eve of WTO accession and the role of financial reforms in the Chinese economy's internationalization process?

The second half of the 1990s was marked by three huge changes:

a) During negotiations with the WTO on China's accession, those who believed China should open up its financial services became more prominent.

b) The Asian financial crisis made people gradually recognize the importance of maintaining stability during the globalization process.

c) China ascended to the Bank for International Settlements. In 1996, sentiment to respecting international rules was getting stronger in China. In response, the Communist Party of China and the central government believed that financial system reform was necessary, and could not be further delayed.

By the end of 1997, the bad debt ratios of the four SOCBs reached 25% while the ratios for self-funding were kept relatively low at 3-4%. Also, Chinese enterprises at that time were very dependent on the SOCBs as their funding came mainly from bank loans, and that the majority were from SOCBs. How to ameliorate the financial situation of these banks became a priority for Chinese authorities.

3) SOCBs' Reforms

Under the aforementioned circumstances, bold reforms on SOCBs were launched, and in 1997 China decided to change banks into real banks. This meant reinforcing the financial supervision function of the PBOC, stimulating the commercialization of SOBs, and building a financial system of multiple layers and categories. With regard to SOCB reforms, China lifted restrictions on the amount of loans, reduced the of savings reserve ratio, injected capital from the Ministry of Finance to the SOCBs, transferred bad debts to asset management companies (AMCs), and separated the operations of the banks' subordinate enterprises and the banks themselves.

4) Reforms After WTO Accession

The reforms after 1997 did not achieve the expected results.

In 2002, discussions began within the government concerning reforms on proprietorship to fundamentally alter the proprietary rights of SOCBs. In 2003, China amended the shareholding policy of SOCBs, and the Chinese government again used measures like injecting public capital, transferring bad debt and using foreign exchange as capital.

This time, Chinese government reform put emphasis on market pressure. One of the highlights was to allow foreign investors to participate to facilitate SOEs' entry overseas markets. The participation of foreign capital was considered a strategic investment because what were sought were not only the capital, but also advanced management techniques, experience and know-how of financial products. It was also expected that entering overseas markets would lead to the adoption of strict accounting systems and the transparent reporting of firms' assets and liabilities.

One of fruits of this round of reforms was ranking Chinese SOCBs behind the three big banks in terms of assets scale in 2005, and being ranked among the top 20 in the world. Furthermore, the bad debt ratios and the capital adequacy ratio (CAR) had been significantly ameliorated for major Chinese SOCBs.

The decline in the SOCBs' bad debt was mainly due to the decline in the NPLs' bad debt ratio by 3.79 percentage points with a 91.5% contribution, while an increase in loans reduced by 0.35 percentage points the bad debt ratio with an 8.5% contribution. With the financial restructuring and 60 billion dollars in newly injected funds, the CAR of the three SOCBs largely improved to 12%, 8.6% and 9.1%, respectively, in 2005.

5) Promise To Foreigners Fulfilled

One of promises made by the Chinese government before the country's WTO accession was that China would open its banking sector on December 11, 2006 to foreign banks registered in China, and the latter shall enjoy the same regulation criteria as Chinese banks.

By September 2006, 25 Chinese cities opened to foreigners in RMB businesses, 111 foreign banking institutions were approved to operate RMB businesses, 73 foreign banks from 22 countries and regions established 191 branches and 61 sub-branches, and 183 banks from 41 countries and regions set up representative offices in 24 Chinese cities. The total assets of foreign banks in China reached as high as 105.1 billion US dollars, or 1.9% of total assets in China's banking sector.

Eight foreign banks applied on December 11, 2006. These were HSBC, Citibank, Standard Chartered Bank, Bank of East Asia, Hang Seng Bank, Mizuho Bank, DBS Bank and Algemene Bank Nederland (ABN).

6) Remaining challenges

China reformed its financial structure and loosened financial restrictions, and the results were encouraging. Nevertheless, compared to the worlds' top banks, the bad debt ratios of Chinese banks remained high, which made it difficult to guarantee the credibility of the banks' assets, and how to treat bad debts that have already been transferred.

The SOCBs' bad debt ratio at around 18% in 2000 was the highest in the world. Japan, a country frequently criticized by the World Bank as an example of poor debt management, had a bad debt ratio of only 10% of GDP. China's four SOCBs had a bad debt of 316 billion RMB, or 20.4% of total loans granted in 1994, and the amount quickly surpassed 1 trillion RMB as an increasing number of SOEs declared bankruptcy in 1996.

Since 2005, the bad debt ratio of SOCBs had dropped below 15%, which is still high by international standards. A 2-3% bad ration is considered a "good" bad debt ratio by international standards, with the world's top 20 big banks having an average bad debt ratio of 3.2%. European banks have a bad debt ration of less than 2%, with US banks even lower than 0.67%.

In terms of profitability, Chinese SOCBs fared poorly, and the adoption of the Basel II highlighted how to reinforce the risk management mechanism and to avoid the accumulation of additional loans for Chinese SOCBs.

China also faces the challenge of how to ameliorate the fund distribution efficiency with the help of interest rates, how to ensure strict corporate governance, how to ensure the executability of laws, how to eliminate corruption, how to liberalize exchange rates and interest rates in the financial markets, and how to compete with foreign banks in the long run.

China continued to have excessive savings, and the restructuring of financial institutions would continue. It is not bad to establish a comprehensive financial institution, but if we want to make this proposal feasible, reforms should be improved, including the legal system and supervision mechanism.

2. WTO-Oriented Credit Restructuring

The credit reform is another essential reform other than the banking reform.

After the establishment of policy banks in 1994, the specialized banks began their commercialization reforms, and the State would end the bureaucratic allocation of credit projects. But the State maintained a strict bureaucratic planning control over the general credit scale, which explains why we can only identify the credit operations of commercial banks during that period as a semi-commercialized one.

Removing direct control over the credit scale of commercial banks was significant as this was a momentous turn in China's credit system evolution. This meant that the commercial banks would have much more authority in making decisions, such as to whom and in how many loans it would grant. What we will discuss is why the credit planning was cancelled and why the credit scale management was cancelled in 1998.

I. Macro and Micro Reasons

This round of reforms from direct regulation to an indirect one signifies a key financial prerequisite to China's accession to the WTO. Other than this, the cancellation was an intrinsic demand for market economy development, and the specific reasons are as follows.

a. The Need For The State Declined

After nearly two decades of reform, the need for the State to maintain credit control declined as the 1990s ended. Financially speaking, the State's fiscal revenues started to have a bigger share in the GDP after the low year of 1995, when public sector debt could be settled through national debt, and the credit substitution function for the national finance gradually declined. In the meantime, with the development of non-State enterprises and the reform of SOEs, the importance of SOEs declined significantly.

Figure 3 shows that the weight of State-owned industrial enterprises dropped below 50% for the first time in 1993 and bottomed out at 31.6% in 1997. There were 84,000 State-owned industrial enterprises in 1978, rising to 99,000 in 1997, an increase of 17.9%. The ratio in the number of SOEs to all national industrial enterprises declined from 24% in 1978 to 18.5% in 1997.

Figure 3: Weight of the State-owned industrial enterprises' Gross Industrial Output Value to all the industrial sector 1978-2004

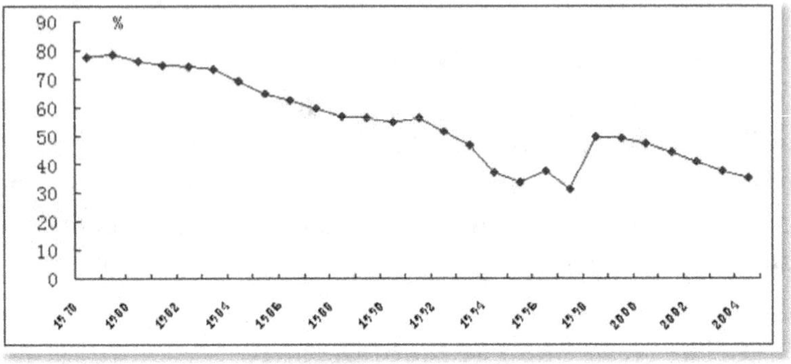

Source: "China Compendium of Statistics: 1949 - 2004", By the Department of Comprehensive Statistics, National Bureau of Statistics

In Figure 3, a sudden reverse in the trend in 1998 seems strange. However, it was due to a change in statistical standards that year. In 1998, the National Bureau of Statistics adopts a new threshold for industrial enterprises, that those to be included in the census shall have at least 5 million RMB in turnover. Being larger in scale than private enterprises, the SOEs' share rose sharply to 49.6% in 1998 with this new statistical threshold.

At the same time, following the "Close down, suspend operations" and "Merge or Shift" measures taken during the reform process, the majority of remaining SOEs were monopolistic firms in the essential sectors, such as electricity, aviation, coal, telecommunications, railways, transportation and petrochemicals. Generally The enterprises in these monopolistic sectors were highly profitable and sufficiently. Thus, after this reform, the number of enterprises needing fresh capital from the State sharply declined. The State did not need to provide bureaucratic planning to the commercial banks to help SOEs obtain loans.

b. The Risks For The State Climbs

With the decline of the need for the State to continue with its traditional credit policy, credit control risks continued to rise because the State's financial control and the budget constraints of the SOBs and SOEs brought the ceaseless accumulation of NPLs, and this accumulation directly threatened China's financial security. Especially when the Asian financial crisis broke out, the Chinese government immediately recognized the urgency to deal with the problem of the NPLs.

The Chinese government gave unprecedented attention to the quality of credit and took initiatives to loosen credit controls by clarifying loan responsibilities in exchange for State non-intervention. This would pave the way for setting responsibilities to the NPLs. The creation of big regional PBOC branches was also one of measures to diminish local governments' intervention in credit.

c. The SOCBs Cherish Loans

Another remarkable trend that emerged is the commercial banks' "loan-cherishing" (or "credit reluctance"). Banks tend to grudge credit to avoid losses due to the change in evaluation criteria with the deepening of financial reforms in China, especially on the eve of its accession to the WTO.

Influenced by the insufficiency of consumption after 1995, the Chinese economy descended continuously until 1997. However, if we look at loans granted by Chinese financial institutions at the end of 1997, the number of RMB loans still grew by 21.3%, which was largely higher than the economy growth.

What was the reason for the economy's downgrade?

I think the real reason was that Chinese commercial banks were unwilling to loan or cherish loans due to their increasingly prudential attitude, because since the Asian financial crisis, the Chinese government started to severely punish those who shirk on their NPL responsibilities, and the punishment could even lead to criminal liability.

The consequences were evident: the growth in RMB loans declined to 15.5% by the end of 1998, and slid even further to 8.3% by the end of 1999. Now that the commercial banks were not willing to grant loans, there was no sense in continuing the adoption of loan scale management.

d. Non-State Economy Needed Credit Support

Since the reform and opening-up, the export processing trade economy and the export-oriented economy occupied a more significant place in the non-State economy. Unfortunately, in the mid 1990s overseas market demand declined. Exports grew by 1.5% in 1996 and 20.5% in 1997, but only 0.4% in 1998 because of fallout from the Asian financial crisis.

The decline in overall demand also affected the non-State economy which only registered a 4.6% growth in industrial output in 1996. That was significantly slower that the growth of over 25% since the reform and opening-up. That squeezed the non-State economy in terms of sales and funding sources. To revitalize the economy, the State needed to develop this important aspect of the national economy and needed the banks to provide more credit to the non-State economy. This justified the loosening of credit controls.

Canceling the credit scale control served as a benchmark for the establishment of the market credit system in China. Since then, credit regained its role as the allocator of financial resources for all economic players. The SOBs were no longer the subsidiaries, substitutes or plain fund suppliers of the National Finance.

In the succeeding years, the SOBs launched their shareholding reform by introducing strategic foreign investors and in launching IPOs. As listed companies, the commercial banks paid more attention to profits due to pressure from public shareholders. At the same time, the remuneration of their executives was linked to profitability.

Comparing to the situation prior to going public, the persistent problem of stimulation was finally solved. The SOBs and their executives paid more attention to their own economic interests rather than the State's efficiency. The SOBs gradually transformed from being scale-oriented to profit-oriented. This transformation had a profound influence on the commercial banks' credit behavior.

II. Two Credit Systems: Administration vs. Market

We have discussed the credit system reform among China's financial reforms. The credit system reform moved from the bureaucratic system based on administrative instructions of the government to the rational system primarily based on market rules. We will compare these two systems to show the immense progress that China had made during the past decades, especially before and after China's accession to the WTO.

a. Market Literatures: Do Not Work In China

The rise in interest rates that accompanied credit restrictions (or the increase in demand for loans with money supply constant) can be restrained by interest ceilings, either those due to the oligopolistic structure of credit markets or due to usury laws. The presence of such ceilings will accentuate the non-price rationing of credit. However, credit rationing only lasted as long as the ceilings were maintained.

Another representative literature on credit rationing was one by Stiglitz and Weiss (1981). They tackled it from the angle of informational asymmetries and reverse choice as the reasons for which credit rationing came into being and functioned, and credit rationing had two scenarios: One was that under similar borrowing conditions, not all obtained funds, even if those who didn't were willing to pay a higher interest rate. Another is that under the given conditions of credit rationing, some borrowers were unable to obtain funds even if they were willing to pay at any interest rate level. But with the increase in credit rationing, they could finally acquire funds.

We can cite other literature on credit operations. However, they all come from Western economics, which largely involved market economies, and were not applicable to China because it was far from being a market economy. Even today, with more than three decades of the reform and opening-up, China is still not a market economy based on European standards.

Their theories have been founded on the basis of the given conditionality and hypotheses such as that of credit rationing, which was defined from the angle of interest rates. The interest rates were marketized, could be used to identify the risks of borrowers, the lenders could choose the borrowers and those suffering from credit rationing was the result of market choice.

b. China Credit Marches Towards Market

Contrary to Western circumstances, China adopted since the reform and opening-up a planned credit system under which credit rationing had a totally different connotation from a market economy. Credit rationing under the planned system could be called "bureaucratic credit rationing" or "administrative credit rationing".

The bureaucratic credit rationing had two characteristics: Interest rates were regulated and loan beneficiaries were determined by the State and not by banks.

When the interest rates were regulated, they could not be taken as a "signal' to identify the borrowers' risks. Under the planned system, the interest rates for loans were artificially driven down by the State, or lower than market rates. They could be even lower than the interest rates for deposits. For example, in 1953 the banks granted loans to State-owned industrial enterprises at a rate of 5.58%, while the interest rate for current deposits in the same period was 5.4% and that for one-year time deposits was 14.4%. No matter what kind of clients the banks would choose, these banks would surely suffer a loss. This could justify why the SOBs were not motivated to filter clients.

When the State determined the loan beneficiaries, banks only served as an operational intermediary agent between the State and their clients. Under the planned system, the SOBs had to grant loans to the sectors and SOEs for projects fully supported by the State, and neither individual firms nor individuals were able to obtain loans from the banks. It was very difficult for non-State-owned enterprises, peasants and individual residents to get financial support from the SOBs. Hence, one major difference between the bureaucratic credit system and a market-based one was that the beneficiaries under the bureaucratic system were a group of working units, i.e. the SOEs, while clients under a market credit system were mostly individual enterprises and residents.

The evolution of China's credit system was a process from the planned credit system towards a market-based credit system. As one part of the evolution of China's banking system reform of the SOBs, it reflected the change in the relationship between the National Finance, the SOEs and the SOBs. The evolution of the credit system brought changes in credit functions transformed gradually from the simple and subordinate role of monetary “distributor” for the National Finance to resource allocator and financing organizer.

The transformation of China’s credit system changed the banks’ credit behavior, and with that, the credit behavior of Chinese SOBs also gradually changed from the bureaucratic or administrative credit towards the market credit system. This change influenced the SOBs’ loan structure, loan scale and allocation efficiency of credit resources. The evolution of China’s credit system is the basis for understanding China’s macro-economic and micro-economic operations.

The efforts of the Chinese government in the aforementioned reforms have been accepted by other economic players in the WTO and were crucial particularly during the global financial crisis.

3. Treatment Of Non-Performing Loans

1) NPLs and Their Treatment

a. 1990s, Decade Of Crises

In the 1990s, the financial crises became more frequent. First there was the Sterling Crisis in 1992, then the Mexico financial crisis erupted in December 1994, and the East Asia financial crisis between 1997 and 1998 was the most serious of all as this crisis quickly spread. In 1998 it reached South Korea which had just joined the OECD (Orgnization for Economics Cooperation and Development). It then spread to South Africa and Russia, and finally crossed the Atlantic in Argentina. Sparked by the US subprime crisis, the global financial crisis erupted in 2008, and this transformed into the sovereign debt crisis in the Eurozone in 2009.

Numerous studies of the 1997 Asian financial crisis and other crises show that one of the common characteristics for these economies is the huge amount of bad debt on the eve of the crises.

The macro economy and micro economy of these countries were fragile before the crises, and this fragility had made these economies endure the pressure from two sides. One is the external pressure generated from the immense amount of short-term foreign debt. Especially in need of compensating the current account deficit, it would be difficult for the economy to be maintained by the inflow of short-term capital, and the slowdown and backspin of capital inflow regardless of reason would extremely weaken the economy and its currency. Another is the internal pressure generated by the weakness in banking supervision, and this had allowed banks, particularly those without sufficient capital, to grant excessively risky loans. When the risks materialized, these banks would not have enough capital to grant new loans and would even face bankruptcy. Thus, when the borrowers were unable to repay their loans, the NPLs would trigger a banking crisis.

b. AMCs, Direct Solution To Crises

To deal with the banking crises, governments, banks and international financial institutions tried to take multiple measures. Their objective was to cope with the immense amount of NPLs in the banking system and to avoid the accumulation of new NPLs.

By the end of the 1980s, the savings and loan institutions in the US were thrown into bankruptcy. To maintain the stability of the financial system, the US government created the Resolution Trust Corporation (RTC) to deal with the NPLs of these institutions. Thus, asset management companies were born.

In the 1990s, especially during the series of financial crises, the NPLs in the banking sector spread across the world. After the US, four European countries (Denmark, Finland, Norway and Sweden) created their own AMCs to restructure their banks' enormous NPLs. Central Europe and Eastern Europe, Latin America and France also took measures measures. Poland founded the Industrial Development Bureau and Mexico the FOBAPROA (Fondo Bancario de Protecciόn al Ahorro or Bank Fund for the Protection of Savings) to stabilize their financial systems.

East Asia and Southeast Asia heavily affected by the crises also established AMCs. These included the Bridge Bank for Japan, the Bureau of Asset Management (KAMCO) for South Korea, the Financial Restructuring Agency (FRA) for Thailand, the Banking Restructuring Agency (IBRA) for Indonesia and the Asset Management Company (Danaharta) for Malaysia.

The AMCs were specific financial institutions created by the State to deal with NPLs in the banking sector. Their mission is specific, and their lifespan is temporary or transitory.

c. Four State-Owned AMCs In China

Under different loan classification systems, NPLs can be defined differently. The US, Japan and Southeast Asian countries have their own NPL solutions, such as the RTC for the US, the Bridge Banks for Japan, South Korean asset management companies and other models for other countries. One common denominator is separating the good from bad banks before being centrally dealt with.

What about China? What has China adopted?

China was the only economy to successfully resist the Asian financial crisis which had swept through Southeast Asia. China's stability contributed to further spreading the financial crisis, which was appreciated by other countries, the World Bank, Asian Development Bank and other international financial institutions.

However, as the pillar of China's financial sector, State-owned banks had accumulated huge amounts of NPLs. PBOC data shows that the NPLs of SOCBs had reached 2.29 trillion RMB on the eve of the creation of four AMCs, and this represented 25.37% of all loans. This threatened the stability and security of the Chinese banking sector.

As previously mentioned, to reduce the bad assets of SOCBs and to prevent the potential risks brought about by these NPLs, the government in 1999 founded four AMCs—China Cinda Asset Management Co., Ltd. (CINDAMC), China Huarong Asset Management Co., Ltd. (CHAMC), China Orient Asset Management Co., Ltd. (COAMC) and China Great Wall Asset Management Co., Ltd. (GWAMCC). They received the bad assets from CCB, ICBC, BOC and ABC. CINDAMC was established in April 1999, and the other three AMCs were created in October 1999.

d. Chinese Model of AMCs

The Regulation on Financial Asset Management Companies promulgated by the State Council on November 10, 2000, stated that the four AMCs were transitory financial institutions specifically established to receive, manage and deal with the NPLs of SOBs, with the government guaranteeing capital.

The regulation also stated that the AMCs will last no more than 10 years. Nevertheless, these AMCs still exist and have even grown. We will discuss this later in the chapter.

The four AMCs are State-owned financial institutions of sole proprietorship and as independent legal persons.

Each of them has the same registered capital of 10 billion RMB from the Ministry of Finance. Their mission is to acquire, manage and treat the bad assets peeled from the four big banks, and to save the assets in reducing losses and addressing financial risks. They bought 1.4 trillion RMB in bad assets, including 405 billion RMB of shares transferred from the debt of 601 SOEs.

The regulation states that the AMCs shall transfer the PBOC re-loans and issue the oriented financial bonds to acquire the banks' NPLs.

While the registered capital of the AMCs was only 10 billion RMB, the amount of NPLs to be treated was 2.29 trillion RMB, or 25.37% of total loans granted. How is it possible for the AMCs to treat the NPLs around 229 times higher than their registered capital?

There were three channels to finance this acquisition: 40 billion RMB as basic fund from the State budget; 570 billion RMB in re-lending from the PBOC; and 820 billion RMB in securities issued by the AMCs towards their respective bank.

e. Dilemma between Policy and Market

China's AMC model in dealing with NPLs has specific characteristics.

As previously mentioned, Chinese AMCs have the independent status of legal persons, special operations targets and a broad business scope. The AMCs are independent because they are positioned by the State as non-banking financial institutions, approved by the State Council, and solely financed by the State, because the targets are not common but policy-oriented, such as the policy acquisition of NPLs of SOBs, the management and treatment of the assets are formed by acquisition of the SOBs' NPLs, broad because they include asset treatment, corporate restructuring, underwriting of securities and mergers and acquisitions, and many of the AMCs' businesses are the same as or equivalent to investment banks.

These specific characteristics make Chinese AMCs also adopt a specific operations model in implementing the strategy between policy guarantee and marketized operations. Government intervention is strong, and the dilemma between policy and market is evident.

f. Policy Guarantee

Because the NPLs of the four big SOCBs are primarily generated by SOEs, the initial purpose of establishing AMCs is to acquire the SOBs' NPLs, to manage and treat the assets accumulated during the acquisition of these NPLs. The State Council shall approve the scope and size of the acquisition, the Ministry of Finance will uniformly disburse the fund, and the AMCs will do everything to reduce losses. Moreover, the AMCs were created during the transition stage from the planned economy to the market economy.

The policy guarantee is the predominant method adopted by Chinese AMCs, and preferential policies have been offered by the State to the AMCs, such as in asset evaluation and tax abatement. That's why Chinese AMCs are also informally called "State-run AMCs". The policy guarantee validates the AMCs' operations and resource allocation. Otherwise, the operations will be disrupted by several non-market factors.

g. Marketized Operations

However, the policy guarantee was not enough, and the AMCs implemented various methods of treating NPLs, including acquiring and dealing with NPLs peeled from commercial banks, debt compensation, asset replacement, transfer and sales, debt restructuring and corporate restructuring, debt-to-equity swaps and phase shareholding, asset securitization, listing recommendations, underwriting of securities and shares, guarantees in the field of assets management, direct investment, bond issuing, commercial borrowing, borrowing from financial institutions and re-loan from the PBOC, investments, financial and legal consultations, asset and project evaluation, corporate audit and bankruptcy liquidation and other businesses approved by financial supervision authorities.

These methods can be ensured by the market rather than guaranteed by government policy. Hence, the marketized operations were adopted to ensure the AMCs' operations.

h. Policy-Market Dilemma

On one hand, there's the government policy guarantee, and on the other, marketized operations. The former is generally called the "visible hand" and the latter the "invisible hand". The combination of policy and the market is not always easy.

The policy guarantee is the precondition for the AMCs' operations. As a special form of financial enterprise, AMCs shall coordinate the common interests of multiple parties in their effort to accomplish multiple goals, such as reducing financial risks, focusing on social stability, and safeguarding State-owned assets. The policy guarantee is needed by AMCs to balance multiple interests, but should not prevent them from implementing a marketized mechanism.

The AMCs shall serve as independent intermediary institutions in their leading role in the comprehensive coordination of society's resources, and counterpoise the interests of related parties in using marketized operations. However, the policy guarantee was only a temporary institutional arrangement to give a hand to the AMCs in the context of China's burgeoning market economy. The guarantee is involved in the initial stage, supervision in the middle and the orientation in the final or sustainable stage of AMCs. It provides a liberal development space in terms of the organizational forms and operational purview of this new type of financial institution.

The AMCs shall combine innovation in business with the innovation in institution, and connect the corporate development model to the sustainable operating capacity of the AMCs. As a completely new financial entity, the AMCs shall explore the operational model and style that suits them best to gain an edge in the market.

The largest challenge for the AMCs in China mainly comes from the de facto incomplete legal environment, such as the right of independent arrangements, equity transfers and capital collaborations, evaluation and tax preferential clauses, and detailed measures on openness to foreign capital.

Fundamentally, the policy guarantee is aimed at creating a relatively liberal environment for the AMCs' marketized operations and to ensure a competitive market environment with sound institutional measures. Obviously, the policy and market faced a real dilemma here.

2) Lifespan of Chinese AMCs

The regulation on financial asset management companies states that the duration of the AMCs shall not exceed 10 years. Why 10 years? Nobody knows. It might have been an impulsive decision as there is no quantitative justification in government documents or academic literature on it.

a. "Popsicle Effect"

However, a "Popsicle Effect" existed when non-performing assets (NPA) were being dealt with. In other words, these assets will lose value at an accelerated rate.

Based on how other countries treated assets, the cashflow follows a parabolic trend. In the first years, the amount gradually rises as personnel gain experience. But as the time goes on, assets which are easy to dispose of and of high value diminish, and the difficulty of dealing with assets also increases. When cashflow peaks, a downward slope begins.

China's AMCs were established in 1999, and were "designed" to last until 2009. However, the "Popsicle Effect" and parabola drove Chinese AMCs to treat the assets as soon as possible, hopefully within the first few years after their creation. They achieved their mission ahead of the deadline.

The AMCs have accomplished their first mission, so why do they still exist?

b. Three Possible Scenarios

Three schools of thought have surfaced on the future of the AMCs after their first mission.

The first argues that the liquidation and cancellation are the solution originally provided by the regulation. Therefore, 10 years after the AMCs were created, they shall be liquidated accordingly. They also argue that the AMCs' mission is to reduce the financial risks and to treat NPLs as soon as possible. Hence, AMCs should focus on adopting multiple measures to liquidate assets through auctions, discounts and package sales. The AMCs hope to liquidate the NPLs within 10 years, the deadline set by the regulation.

The second school advocates the need for AMCs to exist for a long time. Since the AMCs' mission is to preserve the assets and to reduce losses, the strategy shall be to professionally extend the commercial banks' function of asset preservation; hence it won't be necessary to set the AMCs' lifespan and to set an annual cashflow quota to avoid the myopic operations of companies.

The third school tries to combine the first two in arguing that Chinese AMCs have special double mission. These are to reduce the financial risks and to restructure SOEs. To accomplish the double mission, the strategy shall not be one policy for all companies but would depend on the company and assets involved based on a classification of NPAs.

c. Four New Financial Giants

We know that the second school of thought prevailed, and as previously mentioned, the Four Big AMCs not only survived but also grew fast. Today they have become four new financial giants or Four Big new financial institutions 14 years after their creation, which runs counter to the original intent.

According to the Financial Times, CHAMC is working out part of its equity before having the company listed next year. The market has already been awaiting the listing of its competitor, CINDAMC, later this year.

The original intent of the AMCs was to copy the US model in marketizing operations. To our surprise, the Chinese AMC model remains confined to the administrative orientation of the Chinese government with so-called Chinese-specific characteristics, thus making the marketization of Chinese AMCs incompatible with the operations of American RTCs.

The solution that the US adopted in the 1980s to 1990s to deal with the savings and loans crisis was to establish the RTC to deal with NPAs. The RTC operated from 1989 to 1994, its life cycle included the return of bad debts, independent accounting and final liquidation. American RTCs were considered a successful case of how to deal with the NPAs of financial institutions.

It is true that the American RTC was used as the template of NPA treatment in China when the Four Big were founded in 1999. And even Chapter 6, The Termination and Liquidation of the Company, of the Regulation on Financial Asset Management Companies promulgated by the State Council in November 2000 states that when the AMCs are terminated, the Ministry of Finance will organize a team to take charge of liquidation activities. As for the final losses after the AMCs dealt with the NPAs, the Ministry of Finance will submit its recommendations to the State Council for approval.

China's original intent in creating AMCs is similar to that in the US: The AMCs will be abolished after dealing with the NPAs. The Ministry of Finance will manage the liquidation, and outstanding losses will be taken over or assumed by the ministry after approval from the State Council.

d. Chinese Characteristics

The operations of Chinese AMCs are rather strange or had specific Chinese characteristics. On one hand, the bad debts are kept on the account for a long time, and the AMCs were not abolished.

As mentioned earlier, the bad debts absorbed by the Four Big AMCs have as original book value 1.4 trillion RMB or 15% of the total assets of the Four Big banks, while the registered capital of AMCs was only 10 billion RMB provided by the Ministry of Finance, and other financing came from PBOC re-loans and the financial bonds issued by the AMCs: 604.1 billion RMB in re-loans from the PBOC and 811 billion RMB in financial bonds from commercial banks and the State Development Bank.

This specific operation implies that the banks peeled their bad debts first before buying them back in the form of bonds. This financial "game" has made banks unload bad debts, and with just a change of hands, the banks have realized real "win-win". Not only have bad debts of banks been successfully transferred, but the book assets have also augmented the AMCs.

The profits and return of bad debts are essential for both the Ministry of Finance and the repayment of bank loans. However, the cash return rate of the Four Big AMCs in the treatment of NPAs only reached about 20%. It will then be impossible for the AMCs to repay these two financial sources. Among the 1.4 trillion RMB that Four Big banks lent to the Four Big AMCs for the purchase of debt, 800 billion still needed to be repaid.

These loans shall have been repaid in 2009 and 2010. The Ministry of Finance, which is the sole shareholder of the Four Big AMCs, declares the renewal of loans under the same conditions as before. Only 20% of the 1.4 trillion RMB of the NPLs were successfully repaid.

On another hand, the AMCs had no intention to be liquidated. Theoretically speaking, with the listing of large-scale banks, the capital adequacy ratio (CAR) would be raised and the AMCs shall "exit" after completing their original missions.

Contrary to conventional wisdom, the Four Big AMCs started the commercialization in 2007 to expand their business scope and go beyond the acquisition and the treatment of the Four Big bank's NPAs. In 2010, the State Council approved the reform of CINDAMC, which will establish a so-called joint account with the Ministry of Finance.

This account received more than 200 billion RMB in losses due to the NPLs' account holding by CINDAMC in one decade, and this immense amount of peeled losses will have a 10-year duration. In addition, several dozen billion

RMB in re-loans that CINDAMC owed to PBOC will also stop account holding. Hence, the end of the burden of interest rates.

e. China's Fifth AMC

To our surprise, the AMCs managing the NPAs would not die after the treatment of 1.4 trillion RMB. Furthermore, Guoxin Asset Management Co. Ltd. (GUOXINMC) was created in 2010 by the State-Owned Assets Supervision and Administration (SASAC) to drive forward the restructuring of SOEs. This was China's fifth national-level asset management company.

GUOXINMC is solely owned by the SASAC with 20 billion RMB in registered capital (2.95 billion US dollars), whose mission is to transform the small-scale SOEs into profitable enterprises. It will bc focuscd on the domestic sovereign wealth funds and management of State-owned assets. GUOXINMC is similar in this respect with China Investment Corp. which manages part of China's foreign reserves. And it was reported that the first lot of SOEs to be restructured would be the SOEs of national defense. (China Daily, July 28, 2010)

The dysfunction of SOEs in China had multiples symptoms, one of which was the continuous accumulation of NPAs due to the inability of the SOEs to repay the loans granted by SOEs. The dysfunction in the mechanism is evident in the operations of SOEs without even considering the severe corruption within them.

The next question will be: As more and more local and bad debt of large-scale enterprises accumulate, will China also create NPA management companies to take over the local debt?

f. Provincial AMCs

The answer is yes. To reinforce the banks' capacity minimize risks, China's supervision institution had started to strengthen the NPA treatment in the financial field, and the Committee for Banking Supervision of the Ministry of Finance stated in February 2013 that every province could create its own regional asset management company to take charge of acquiring and treating NPLs generated by local financial institutions. (Reuters, February 18, 2013)

This decision was phenomenal because it was the first time for the Chinese government to allow the establishment of AMCs at the provincial level, and this would complicate the asset management market in China and change the market scenario. Prior to that, the financial NPA transfer market was monopolized by the Four Big AMCs.

According to data from the China Banking Regulatory Commission (CBRC), the NPL rate of Chinese banks rebounded in the third quarter (0.95%) to 0.98% at the end of the previous year. The NPL rates for the first, second and third quarters were 0.94%, 0.94% and 0.95%, respectively. Another report shows that in 2012, the new NPLs of commercial banks increased at less than 10% on a year-to-year basis. Influenced by the constraints of Basel II, the commercial banks faced higher requirements in terms of CAR, and the treatment of NPLs would also face additional time pressure. (2012 Market Investigation Report of Financial NPA Market in China, China Orient Asset Management Co., Ltd.)

Faced by the ascending cycle of NPLs of the banking sector, supervision authorities started to drive local governments to participate in the NPA treatment and to accelerate the NPAs' rotation in financial institutions.

This notice complemented the Administrative Measures for the Transfer of State-Owned Assets of Financial

Enterprises, No. 52 Document of the Ministry of Finance issued in February 2013. It was meant to clarify the scope of NPA acquisition by the AMCs to be created or authorized by local governments and to encourage local governments to boost the transfer of NPAs within their jurisdiction.

The difference between national AMCs and provincial or local AMCs was that the AMCs or operating companies established or authorized by local governments of provinces, autonomous regions and municipalities directly under the central government was they were only allowed to acquire the NPAs of financial enterprises at the level of their respective areas, while the Four Big AMCs acquired the NPAs of financial institutions at the national level.

This new policy shattered the market monopoly in the growing market power in the NPA treatment. The intervention and coordination of local governments would activate the transaction of more NPA packages in which most come from SOEs, and the new local government AMCs would help solve the problem of pricing difficulty and low return rate of NPAs.

Furthermore, since the monopoly of the treatment market would be shattered and the market would be activated with the participation of more players, the AMCs created for the purpose of acquiring and treating the NPAs of commercial banks would also see their businesses increase when the treatment market develops.

4. Opening up to Foreign Competition

Opening up to foreign competition was not only a requirement of the WTO but also necessary for the Chinese government to continue to boost its reform and opening-up policy. And among multiple WTO-oriented policies, the opening-up to foreign competition in the treatment of NPAs was an essential step.

1) Intervention of Foreign Capital

On May 29, 2003, Liu Mingkang, newly nominated CBRC chairman, announced that the NPA rate was still as high as 24.13%, and expected it to be reduced by 3 or 4 percentage points that year. The "first oath" of Liu was based on the "pledge" that China had made for WTO accession in terms of the NPA rate—to make it less than 10%.

The efforts of the Four Big AMCs were appreciated. However, the problem is that once one lot of NPAs is treated, another one grows, and it follows a vicious cycle. Hence, the intervention of foreign capital was necessary also because of the lack of experience of Chinese institutions such as the AMCs in dealing with NPAs.

a. Goldman Sachs

The US model is something that China will learn from in the initial stage of NPL restructuring. The Goldman Sachs Group (GS), one of world's strongest players, was one such example. That's because it had treated dozens of billions of dollars in NPAs during the 1980s and 1990s. Since the turn of the century, GS took over major NPAs of Japan and South Korea and became the largest transnational bank as NPA treatment operator in these two countries. GS is also the main bank for treating NPAs in Southeast Asia.

What the NPA treatment requires most is not funds but experience and management. NPA treatment was a totally new field for China because there was no precedent to copy, no legal stipulation to adopt and no second market to operate in. All these impeded on the development of China's NPA treatment. That's why GS was chosen as one of first foreign players to be introduced in China in treating NPAs.

b. Morgan Stanley

Another important foreign player in the field of NPA treatment is Morgan Stanley (MS), which considers the NPAs as something of great value. Hence, it was quickly attracted by China's opening up of the NPA market to foreign companies.

To regulate the entry of foreign capital in the restructuring and disposal of assets by financial asset management companies, the Interim Provisions on Absorption of Foreign Capital Financial Asset Management Companies to Participate in Asset Restructuring and Disposal was promulgated by the Ministry of Foreign Trade and Economic Cooperation, the Ministry of Finance and PBOC on and effective as of October 26, 2001. This is a real watershed document in the development process of asset restructuring as it stipulates that "Asset management companies may absorb foreign capital to restructure and dispose of assets owned by them". (See Article 2, Interim Provisions on Absorption of Foreign Capital Financial Asset Management Companies to Participate in Asset Restructuring and Disposal, October 26, 2001)

c. One Joint-Venture with CHAMC

Only a month since the first public bidding conference was organized by CHAMC on the foreign institutions' NPA treatment, the MS won an asset package of 10.8 billion RMB. After the initial success of MS in China, the MS formed a joint venture (JV) of AMCs with CHAMC.

According to their agreement, MS would pay CHAMC $117 million in cash, and in the following two years, MS would invest in the JV company 25% of the cash to be returned from the NPA treatment, then the profits would be shared equally with CHAMC. The minimum return rate of CHAMC could reach 21%, in which 50% would be paid in cash and another 50% would be invested in the JV company. If the returned value from the NPA treatment is less than 190% of the amount contributed, the division of profits would be 80% for the Chinese party and 20% for the foreign party. Anything over 190% would be an even split in profits.

In the second public bidding conference organized by CHAMC in the first half of 2003, MS was particularly interested in more than 20 billion RMB of the NPA package of CHAMC in the Guangdong area. MS was granted the QFII (Qualified Foreign Institutional Investor) by the CSRC.

d. Another Joint-Venture with CCB

Faced with the irresistible temptation of China's NPA market and with the QFII, MS was considering close collaborations with other Chinese institutions to accelerate its penetration in China. The most competitive candidate in the eyes of MS was China Construction Bank (CCB), which stood out from the rest of the financial institutions in May 2002 in the field of NPA "body-shaping" activities.

CCB's performance was also encouraging: By the first semester of 2003, CCB's NPL rate had reached 14.05% based on the five-grade classification—that is to say, the CCB had accomplished in 2003 the bottom line of 2005.

MS adopted a similar strategy with CCB by setting up a JV company, and the CCB implemented a policy of "Sales + Profit-Sharing in Collaboration" in introducing MS during the treatment process to around 4.3 billion RMB in NPAs from the branches from Jiangsu Province, Zhejiang Province and Shanghai. This policy was similar to the treatment mode with CHAMC which sold to MS a package of 10.8 billion RMB.

Under the policy, the CCB would sell 70% of assets to MS, and the two would treat the remaining 30% in the form of a JV company with shared profits. This JV includes one company of asset owners and one company of assets service to manage and jointly treat the asset packages. The treatment would require from three to five years.

This policy was the optimal solution for the Chinese bank at that time to realize the maximization of returned profits in avoiding the difficulties of pricing and the losses of State-owned assets. The policy helped the CCB get rid of heavy historical burden and to go light to the market.

e. Win-Win for MS and CCB

After the establishment of a JV with CCB, MS and the CCB signed the "Pilot Project of NPA Treatment" in Beijing on July 9, 2003. This was the very first time for a Chinese commercial bank to collaborate with foreign capital in the field of NPA treatments, and this was also the first time for MS to adopt the "One-to-One" mode in the Chinese NPAs market to acquire the NPAs of SOCBs.

The CCB will, through the collaboration with MS, capitalize on MS' international advanced techniques and experiences in the NPAs treatment to improve CCB's management skills in handling NPAs and to explore new channels of the NPA treatment. MS would also provide the CCB investment management training in the treatment and securitization of NPAs.

Hence, the JV between MS and the CCB was a typical "win-win" collaboration model. The Four Big AMCs held almost 1.4 trillion RMB in NPAs and an enormous supply of other NPAs to be peeled, and MS could make use of their advantages in capital and resources and in treatment experience. On the 4 billion RMB package, the CCB would evaluate the NPAs to be sold to the establishment of a JV by liquidizing the NPA package.

Suppose that the basis was 100 million RMB of the NPAs and that the discount negotiated by the CCB with the MS was 50%, then the CCB would get 50 million RMB. The CCB can at least grant loans with this money. For its part, MS could restructure listed companies or package the companies to be listed, and the reformed NPAs would then be listed in the market.

There are fundamental differences between foreign NPAs and Chinese NPAs. Generally speaking, the former is generated by cyclical recessions in the economy while the latter is based on multiple complicated factors, including reform and system transformation and SOE bankruptcies. Because of a lack of prudence in policymaking, some projects had to be suspended later. And because of a lack of capital, some projects which depended entirely on bank loans created big risks for projects.

Therefore, Chinese NPAs shall be differentiated with a more detailed methodology. One portion of the assets could not operate anymore because of a lack of liquidity, and this lack would have a negative influence on the normal operation of enterprise. That results in bad debts. These NPAs have a huge value for potential investors because injecting them with capital would make them function properly.

Of course, the uniqueness of Chinese NPAs is important. What attracts foreign investors to Chinese NPAs? We will them in the eyes of foreigners to complete the differentiation discussion from another angle.

2) Interaction between Foreign Investors and Local Market

a. NPAs—a Cyclical Puzzle for China

As previously mentioned, 1.4 trillion RMB ($170 billion) in NPAs have been peeled from the Four Big SOCBs to the four AMCs for treatment. This helped the Four Big banks ameliorate their NPA rates and explore a new market. And almost daily, Chinese banks or the government announce a reduced NPA ratio.

Nevertheless, the NPAs remain a thorny problem for the Chinese banking sector because the peeling in 1999 has not transferred all the problem loans of the banking sector to the newly created AMCs, and the commercial banks continue to stockpile a huge amount of NPAs. Another lot of peeling happened in 2004. 330 billion RMB ($40 billion) was peeled from three SOBs to the China Cinda Asset Management Co., Ltd. Estimates show the NPAs in 2004 reached nearly 4.13 trillion RMB ($500 billion), which put China second only to Japan in NPA terms.

b. Categories of Investors

What kind of foreign investors were interested in Chinese NPA treatment? A May 2005 PriceWaterhouseCoopers investigation conducted in China involving 17 institutions shows that 82% were the NPA-related departments of banks or investment banks, or investment funds of non-performing equity. Others included one investment company, one commercial bank and one direct investment company. Fifty-three percent were located in the US and 23% in Hong Kong.

This result was not surprising because the majority of banks or investment banks with specific department for NPAs are based in the US. Most of institutions invest in other countries or regions in Asia. However, more and more small and medium scale Hong Kong and US investment funds participate or intend to invest in the NPA treatment market of different sectors and regions. Other than the Chinese Mainland, 94% have invested in at least in one country or region's NPAs, and 65% have acquired NPAs in at least in one Asian country or region.

Figure 4: Transactions approved or to be approved in Chinese Market

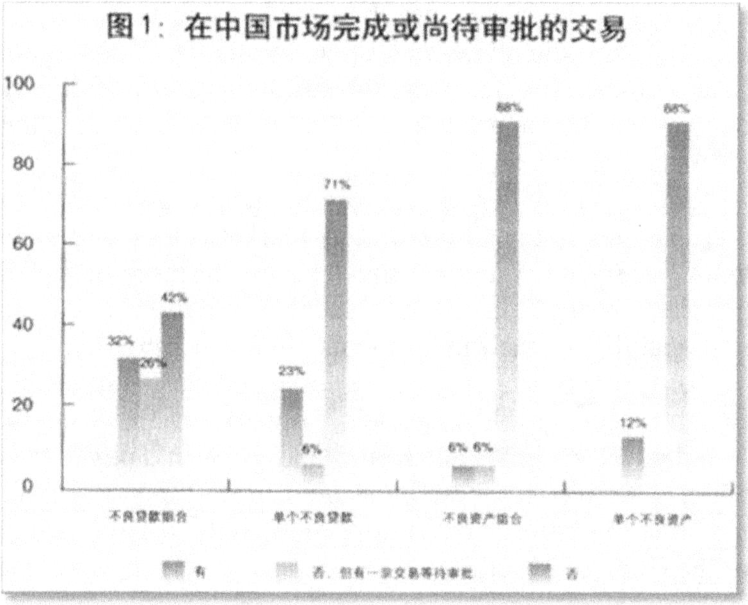

Portfolio of NPL Individual NPL Portfolio of NPL Individual NPL
Yes No, but with one transaction to be approved No
(From left to right respectively)
Source: PricewaterhouseCoopers (PWC), May 2005.

The NPA market blossomed following the savings and loan crisis in the US towards the end of the 1980s. In 1997, when the devaluation of the Thai baht triggered the Asian financial crisis, investors in the US NPA market realized that Asian NPAs and other non-performing equities had a huge investment potential. They then established offices in Thailand, Indonesia, South Korea and Japan.

Thanks to the efforts of these investors, the NPA market in these countries flourished from 1998 to 2002. And when the NPAs in the markets of these economies were coming to an end, new NPA markets in the Chinese Mainland and Chinese Taiwan region were created.

Figure 4 shows that 58% of samples had at least one transaction in the Chinese Mainland. This result is not surprising neither because big NPA projects were not common, nor the auction of assets by the CCB was a rare case. Another problem was the difficulty and uncertainty in discovering appropriate NPA projects and treating individual assets.

With regard to personnel, 56% of samples assigned 1 to 5 employees in the Chinese NPA market, 11 to 20 people among 38% of samples and 19% with more than 20 people. Many investors spent heavily, but the sustainability of their investments remained a problem.

Forty-five percent of samples assigned staff responsible for the Chinese NPA market to work in the Chinese Mainland, 29% in Hong Kong, and 16% in Tokyo. It is understandable that these investors needed time to observe the situation before committing more staff to Hong Kong or the Chinese Mainland.

c. NPL/NPA Packages Preferred

After the analyses of investors' categories, we will try to find multiple preferences of investors who are already interested in Chinese NPA treatment. Which sort of packages will investors choose—large, medium or small-scale asset packages?

Figure 5, NPL/NPA Packages preferred, shows that medium-scale asset packages are the most preferred

(49%), although as previously mentioned 58% of samples have indicated that they prefer large-scale asset packages, and we see that asset packages are more attractive than individual assets for foreign investors.

Figure 5: NPL/NPA Packages Preferred By Investors

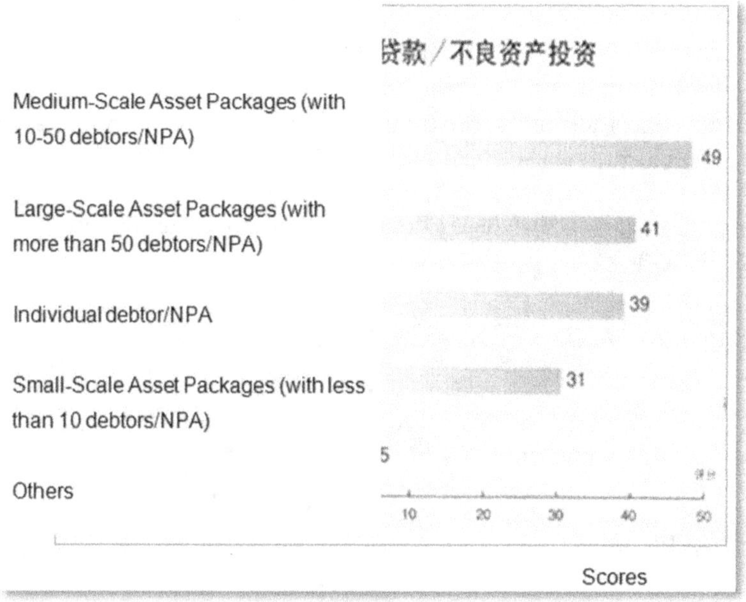

Source: PricewaterhouseCoopers (PWC), May 2005.

The asset packages are more appreciated because the potential investors can find more potential opportunities to achieve a greater return of investment. Empirically speaking, large-scale asset packages are appreciated particularly by senior investors while new investors are more inclined to acquire small-scale asset packages. Individual asset packages are more appreciated probably because the individual assets give an impression that their risks are lower while their profit-generating capacity is higher.

d. Investment Scales Preferred

After NPL/NPA Packages Preferred', we move to Figure 6, Investment Scales preferred, which shows that the overwhelming majority of samples (92%) are inclined to invest in projects worth over $5 million (based on the acquisition price). Among the 92%, 38% prefer investment scales of between $ 6-20 million, 31% prefer those between $ 21-50 million, and 23% prefer projects over $ 50 million. The findings support the fact previously mentioned that large- and medium-scale asset packages are most appreciated by foreign investors.

Figure 6: Investment Scales Preferred Calculated On The Basis Of Individual NPL/NPA Projects

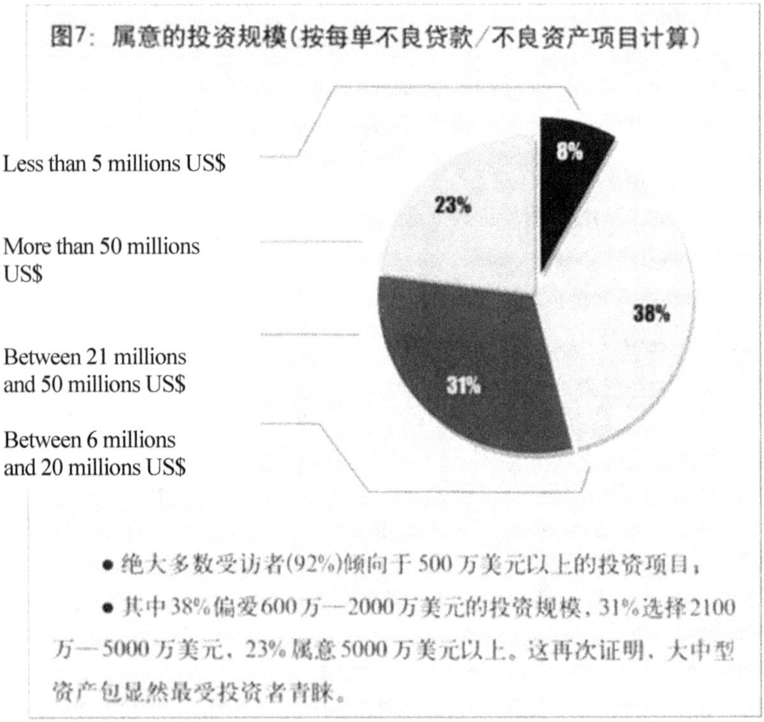

Source: PricewaterhouseCoopers (PWC), May 2005.

Looking ahead, 23% want to invest within 1 to 2 years in four projects between $ 6-20 million per year, and another 23% are ready to invest in three to four projects between $ 4-50 million, and 14% want three to four projects over $ 50 million. Clearly, foreign investors prefer large-scale NPA transactions in China.

e. Preferred Locations Of NPL/NPA

Figure 7 shows the Preferred Locations of NPLs/NPAs.

Figure 7: Five Preferred Locations of NPL/NPA

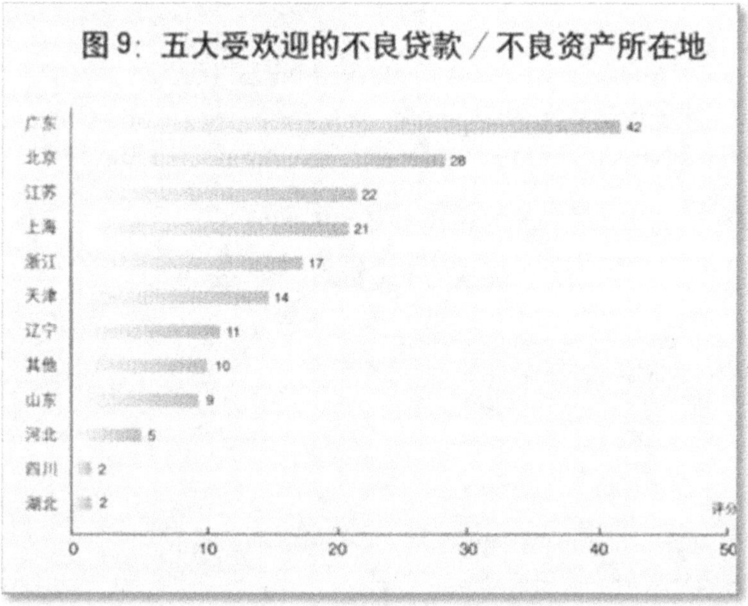

Guangdong Province, Beijing City, Jiangsu Province, Shanghai City, Zhejiang Province, Tianjin City, Liaoning Province, Others, Shandong Province, Hebei Province, Sichuan Province and Hubei Province

Scores

(From top to bottom respectively).
Source: PricewaterhouseCoopers (PWC), May 2005.

It shows the five favorite locations where NPAs are located. These are Guangdong Province, Beijing, Jiangsu

Province, Shanghai and Zhejiang Province. Potential investors prefer coastal and more developed provinces/cities.

Guangdong tops the list because of its relatively advanced economic development level and its proximity to Hong Kong. Beijing and Shanghai are among the top 5 locations (second and fourth, respectively) because they are the political and commercial centers, respectively, and their unique status ensures investors, especially foreign investors in the treatment of thorny types of NPAs in China. While Zhejiang and Jiangsu are not traditional hot markets, their high ranking is not surprising due to their long history of a "culture of commerce".

f. Characteristics Of Preferred NPL/NPA

What are the specific characteristics of Chinese NPLs/NPAs preferred by foreign investors? (See Figure 8)

Figure 8: Categories Of Preferred NPL/NPA

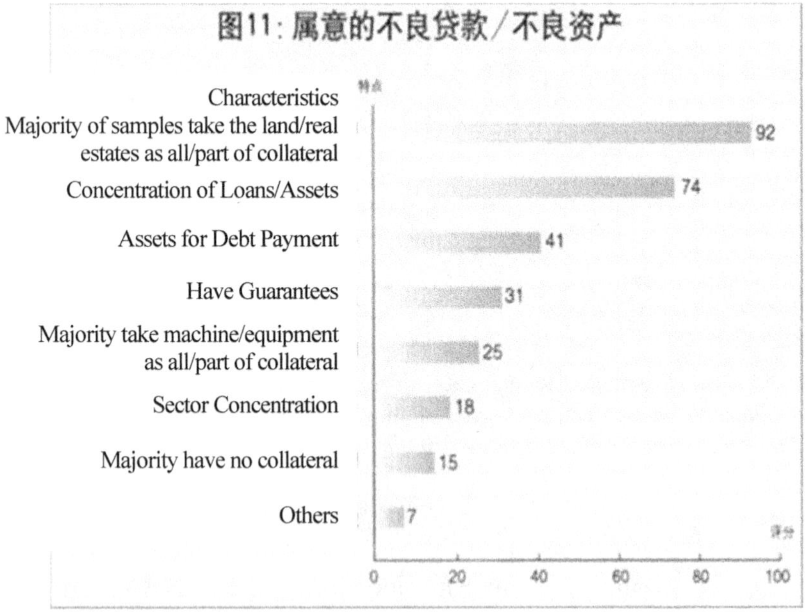

Source: PricewaterhouseCoopers (PWC), May 2005. The preferred NPLs/NPAs have four major characteristics:

a) They are collateralized by land/real estate. The reason is rather obvious because the properties can be priced and easily sold, if necessary. In reality the hypothecation is in most cases just taken as part of negotiations, while the forced execution of mortgages, though clearly provided by law, has rarely taken place probably because it is more of a commercial threat than a legal tool, and also because it is difficult to find an appropriate buyer of this sort of hypothecated property in China.

b) They offer common or proximity locations. This space concentration will help the supervision and management of loans and assets, facilitate the selling of loans and assets by investors, and help investors increase their profit and reduce the cost of loan and asset operations.

c) These assets are the assets for debt payment which are received by the bank to countervail correspondent debt. Some potential investors prefer assets for debt payment because this sort of treatment is through sales, hence more certain and explicit. Nevertheless, other factors will make it more difficult to sell the assets for debt payment, such as the ambiguity of property rights and invisible debts, among others. That's why other potential investors take a prudent attitude towards the assets for debt payment.

d) These NPLs/NPAs have guarantees. But this is true only for a small part of assets because it is almost impossible for foreign investors to have access to the information of warrantors so as to execute and obtain the assets or warrantors.

g. Expected Internal Rate of Return (IRR)

We move on to the pre-tax Internal Rate of Return (IRR) that potential foreign investors expect with regard to NPL/NPA treatment operations. (See Figure 9)

Figure 9: Expected Internal Rate of Return (IRR)

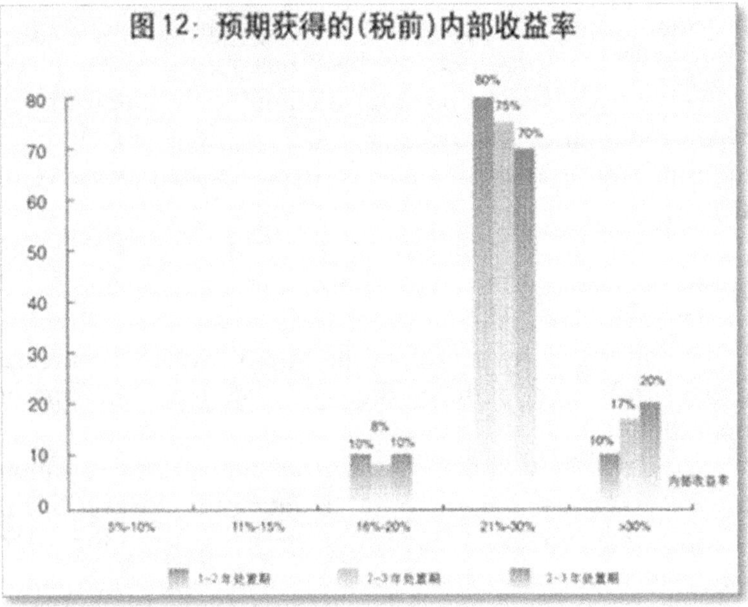

1 to 2 year treatment period 2 to 3 year treatment period 2 to 3 year treatment period Internal Return Rate (IRR) (From left to right). Source: PricewaterhouseCoopers (PWC), May 2005.

The majority of foreign investors expected an IRR of between 21% and 30% which is normal in other countries and regions during the process of NPL/NPA treatment. However, this IRR is too high for China because it largely exceeds the IRR that Chinese sellers of NPLs/NPAs had preset. Therefore, the transactions will be less easy due to the difficulties for two or more parties to reach a consensus.

h. Preferred Investment Strategies

What kind of strategies will potential investors adopt when they acquire the focused asset packages? (See Figure 10)

Figure 10: Preferred Investment Strategies

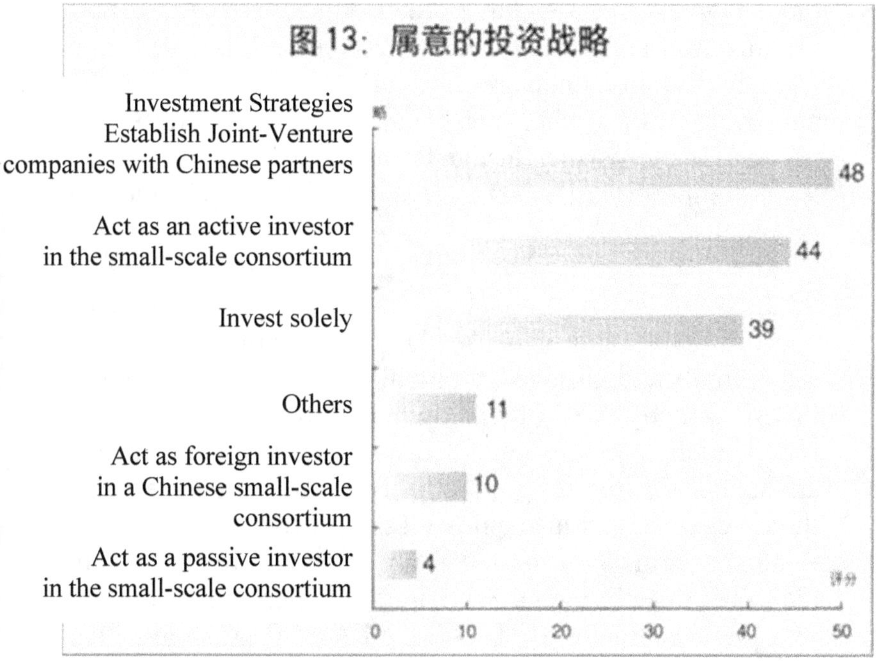

Source:PricewaterhouseCoopers (PWC), May 2005.

Figure 10 shows that the most appreciated investment modes include establishing joint venture companies with Chinese partners to play an active role in the small-scale consortium.

JVs are the first choice for foreign buyers to invest in Chinese NPA treatment market because most foreign investors realize that it is crucial to establish a relationship with local sources and authorities, especially during the approval process of projects, with other creditors and enterprise staff.

Furthermore, JVs are also a more cost-effective channel for foreign buyers to penetrate into the Chinese market than investing by themselves. Sometimes, JVs are also required by Chinese NPL/NPA sellers to participate in the bid. However, JVs have their disadvantages. Their organization and structure are relatively complicated, and specific requirements are normally imposed to get the approval from authorities. Hence, greater efforts are needed. If the partner in the JV takes charge of repaying loans, supervise its activities will be a complicated problem.

The experiences show that new investors are often inclined to play an active role in the small-scale consortium as they can use the consortium to share the risks, funds and knowledge than those who have chosen to invest directly with their own return operation team. Independent and absolute decision-making is the major advantage for investing directly. In assuming all the risks, the investors enjoy also enjoy all the profits.

In addition, 87% of the samples have already or are planning to collaborate with local Chinese investors for the joint acquisition of NPLs/NPAs. This shows that foreign investors recognize the importance of local knowledge and liaisons.

i. Foreign Expectations from Chinese Partners

We turn to what foreign investors expect from their Chinese partners.

Foreign investors hope to get local partners to assist them in identifying projects, repay loans and engage in due diligence. Foreign investors expect their local partners to explore and identify NPA packages, and this requires their local partners to have a focused relationship in the NPA package identification.

Figure 11: Foreign Expectations from Chinese Partners

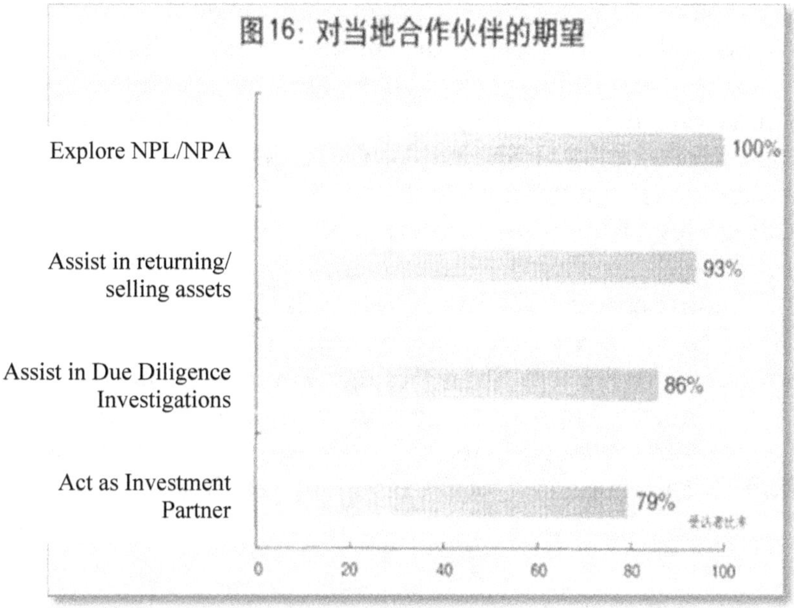

Characteristics

Ratio of Samples

Source: PricewaterhouseCoopers (PWC), May 2005.

Figure 11 shows that almost all samples (93%) hope their local partners will assist them in loan payments because with a local network. And 86% expect their local partners to conduct due diligence investigations as foreign investors said their local partners often keep confidential information of loans/assets, and this can help foreign investors better evaluate the return potential of NPLs/NPAs.

As the Chinese legislation landscape is not only complicated but also evolving rapidly, and debtor files are rarely accessible, it is good to depend on people involved in selling assets. By accumulating experience and knowledge, investors will depend less and less on sellers. Supervising sellers remains a problem, and foreign investors would normally recruit a professional accounting firm to serve as supervisor and project manager.

Just like other problems during three decades of reforms and opening-up, the NPAs are a vicious cycle for China due to the repetitive nature of new NPLs/NPAs. And in order to deal with NPLs/NPAs, the entry of foreign investors is inevitable. We have carefully analyzed the Categories of Investors, Preferred NPL/NPA Packages by Investors, Preferred Investment Scales, Preferred Locations of NPLs/NPAs, Preferred Characteristics of NPLs/NPAs, Expected Internal Rate of Return (IRR), Preferred Investment Strategies and Foreign Expectations from Chinese Partners to provide a realistic scenario of interactions between foreign investors, the Chinese NPL/NPA market and local Chinese players in this field.

CHAPTER 2

Finance & Real Estate Reforms

"It is not the strongest of the species that survive, nor the most intelligent, but the one most responsive to change." (Scopes Monkey Trial, Clarence Darrow, 1925)

INTRODUCTION

This chapter starts with a quote from Clarence Darrow. Some hated, but others loved the global financial crisis. The Chinese mainland (People's Republic of China, "China" hereafter) is among several economies fared relatively better against this crisis. However, as Chinese often say, "*China has also its own problems*". One of them is housing.

With economic growth and financial development factors, China's real estate reforms had solid economic and financial foundation. Among the financial factors, savings growth is crucial. The relationship between finance and real estate reforms is bi-directional: Finance ensures and stimulates housing reform, and housing reform impulses finance in turn.

SECTION 1 REAL ESTATE REFORMS

Let's review the housing reform history in China during the last three decades.

1. Historical Background

After the Communist Party took power in 1949, the Chinese government started to adopt the socialist planned economy. According to the Constitution, all land and housing resources belonged to the state in a broad sense, including governments at different levels from Beijing (central government) to provinces or autonomous regions or municipalities directly under the central government, to counties, to different local public entities and *Danwei* (work units). Under this planned economy, laws in China regard ownership of buildings as separate from land. We had to wait 37 years to finally see the birth of the first Chinese land law, the Law of Land Administration of the People's Republic of China (June 25, 1986). Before housing reform, no building could be sold or bought which, in fact, did not exist at all.

The housing system under such a planned economy was also a planned housing system: Housing adopted a government-funded and government-run system. According to Fan H.S. (1999): Public housing fell into two categories during the planned economy era: Directly managed housing implemented by the local government housing administration, and self-managed housing built, distributed and managed by State-owned enterprises and institutions for their employees and families.

Hence, urban housing supply and conditions before housing reform largely depended on two factors - either State represented by different levels of government invested with the state budget, or individual *Danwei* invested if the *Danwei* you were bound to was well situated and had a healthy financial situation.

This system was called the welfare-oriented public housing distribution system which dominated across China in the planned economy. Under this system, the distribution of housing was based (theoretically) on a package of variables for all the employees, such as family members, age, gender, administrative position, technical grade, Party membership or not, professional performance or contributions during their service for *Danwei*.

Figure 12: Monthly Housing Rent In Beijing Region 1950-1979

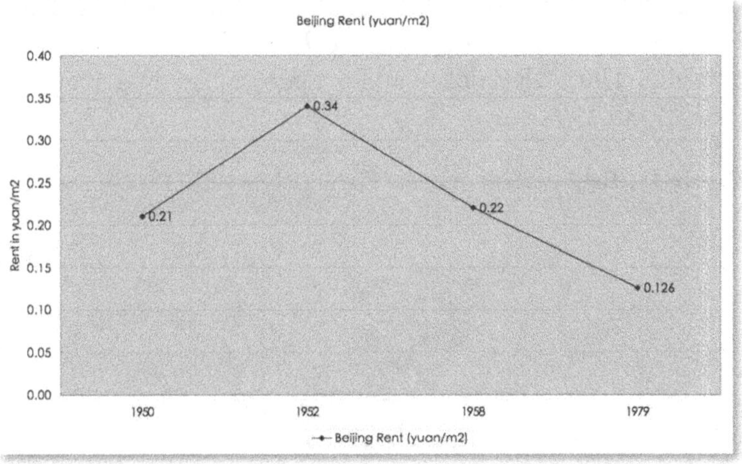

Sources: Survey of Rent on 1783 Households' in 1953 by Beijing Real Estate Administration Bureau, and other statistics of this Bureau; "Thinking about the Housing Reform Process in China" (Fu B., 1997)

How about the rent in that period? As housing was regarded as welfare which was one of characteristics of Chinese socialism or communism, Chinese urban families did pay something at the start of the New China, but paid less and less in time since 1958.

As depicted in Figure 12, the peak in the rental trend was 1952 at 0.34 RMB/m2 which was 60% higher than in

1950. In July 1952, the Rent Standard for the Public Housing was amended. In 1958, Beijing started to implement the new Rent Standard for Public Housing for Civil Use. Rent continued to decrease to 0.22 RMB/m2 in 1958. This downward trend prevailed until 1979 to 0.126 RMB/m2.[1].

The following figure depicts the Beijing Rent-Income Ratio (RIR) from 1952 to 1992. Just like Figure 12, 1953 was also the peak at 9.27%, 1.79% higher than the previous year. However, the trend started to drop to 6.15% in 1958 due to the same reason as in Figure 12, and continued to decrease to 1.93% in 1978, the year when the economic reform was launched in China, Beijing urban families spent on average only 1.93% of their total income on rent. The RIR continued to decrease to less than 1% (0.73%) in 1992.

Figure 13: Beijing Rent-Income Ratio (RIR) 1952-1992

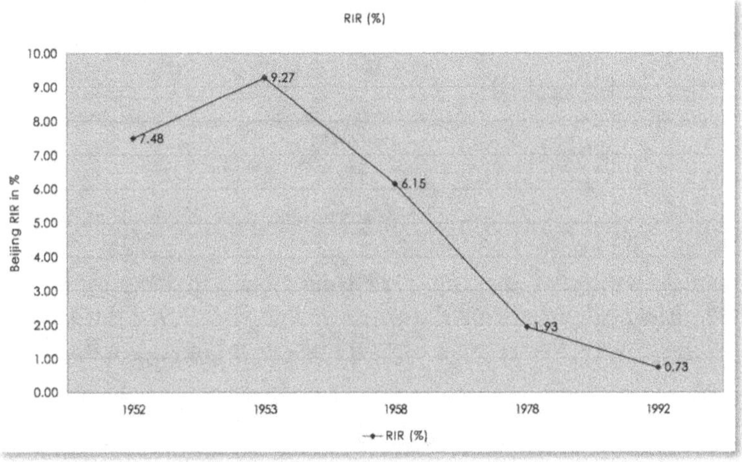

Sources: Idem with Figure 12

[1] Source: 'Survey of Rent on 1783 Households', 1953, Beijing Real Estate Administration Bureau, and other statistics of this Bureau.

We have tried to discover a similar survey on rent in China. Unfortunately, we could only find dispersed figures from other regions, and complete China data was unavailable. In fact, Beijing is just a city, not a specific one in terms of rent, and we have not found specific housing policies for Beijing. Hence, Beijing can be representative of China during that period of time.

The Chinese government fixed the RIR at 7.48% in 1951 (J. G. LI et al., 2007). This corresponds to the scenario in Beijing. At the start of the 1950s, a part of Chinese public housing adopted the policy, "Maintain housing with its rent" (J. ZHANG et al., 1992). Generally speaking, the RIR was estimated at around 10% (X. X. MIN et al., 1999) on average in that period, which is only slightly higher than the RIR in Beijing.

Nevertheless, influenced by excessive emphasis on the importance of welfare housing, the "Maintain housing with its rent" policy was neglected and even denied after 1956. In 1963, the per square meter rent for public housing dropped even further to 0.10 RMB/m2, and the RIR was only 2-3% (B. LI, 2009).

Influenced by the necessity to incarnate "Socialist Superiority" during the Cultural Revolution, the rent standard for public housing in all big Chinese cities went out of control. The RIR was 2-3% on average in 1975, and fell to 1.92% in 1978 on the eve of the reform (China Statistical Yearbook, 1992). Finally, the "Low rent plus high subsidies" or "Symbolic rent" policy[2] replaced the "Maintain housing with its rent" policy, and became a standard for all urban public housing in China.

[2] 'Symbolic rent' policy: tenants pay only a minuscule amount of money just to demonstrate their leasing relationship with lessors who are the State or its representative institutions.

Table 3: Per Capita Annual Income and Engel's Coefficient of Urban and Rural Households

Year	Per Capita Annual Disposable Income of Urban Households		Per Capita Annual Net Income of Rural Households		Engel's Coefficient of Urban Households	Engel's Coefficient of Rural Households
	Value (RMB)	Index	Value (RMB)	Index	(%)	(%)
1978	343.4	100.0	133.6	100.0	57.5	67.7
1979	405.0	115.7	160.2	119.2		64.0
1980	477.6	127.0	191.3	139.0	56.9	61.8
1981	500.4	129.9	223.4	160.4	56.7	59.9
1982	535.3	136.3	270.1	192.3	58.6	60.7
1983	564.6	141.5	309.8	219.6	59.2	59.4
1984	652.1	158.7	355.3	249.5	58.0	59.2
1985	739.1	160.4	397.6	268.9	53.3	57.8
1986	900.9	182.7	423.8	277.6	52.4	56.4
1987	1002.1	186.8	462.6	292.0	53.5	55.8
1988	1180.2	182.3	544.9	310.7	51.4	54.0
1989	1373.9	182.5	601.5	305.7	54.5	54.8
1990	1510.2	198.1	686.3	311.2	54.2	58.8
1991	1700.6	212.4	708.6	317.4	53.8	57.6
1992	2026.6	232.9	784.0	336.2	53.0	57.6
1993	2577.4	255.1	921.6	346.9	50.3	58.1
1994	3496.2	276.8	1221.0	364.3	50.0	58.9
1995	4283.0	290.3	1577.7	383.6	50.1	58.6
1996	4838.9	301.6	1926.1	418.1	48.8	56.3
1997	5160.3	311.9	2090.1	437.3	46.6	55.1
1998	5425.1	329.9	2162.0	456.1	44.7	53.4
1999	5854.0	360.6	2210.3	473.5	42.1	52.6
2000	6280.0	383.7	2253.4	483.4	39.4	49.1
2001	6859.6	416.3	2366.4	503.7	38.2	47.7
2002	7702.8	472.1	2475.6	527.9	37.7	46.2
2003	8472.2	514.6	2622.2	550.6	37.1	45.6
2004	9421.6	554.2	2936.4	588.0	37.7	47.2
2005	10493.0	607.4	3254.9	624.5	36.7	45.5

2006	11759.5	670.7	3587.0	670.7	35.8	43.0
2007	13785.8	752.5	4140.4	734.4	36.3	43.1
2008	15780.8	815.7	4760.6	793.2	37.9	43.7
2009	17174.7	895.4	5153.2	860.6	36.5	41.0
2010	19109.4	965.2	5919.0	954.4	35.7	41.1
2011	21809.8	1046.3	6977.3	1063.2	36.3	40.4
2012	24564.7	1146.7	7916.6	1176.9	36.2	39.3

Source: Table 11-2, China National Statistical Yearbook 2013

Suppose we are in a static state where the revenue is constant and the proportion of revenue for paying food plus rent is also constant, then rent will rise if food consumption drops, and vice versa. With quick economic growth in China, the proportion of revenue spent on food had fallen. Therefore, Chinese inhabitants could have more disposable income to pay for rent. The proportion of rent expenditures depends also on the evolution of rent in the housing market and salary fluctuations.

The relationship between the Engels' Coefficient and RIR is not so simple in the real world, since other factors such as government subsidies shall also be considered. Otherwise, the comparison would be difficult, even impossible.

For instance, in 1977 expenses for housing (family facilities, water and electricity not included) occupied 15.3% of all expenses in the US, 9.8% for medical care and 1.6% for education. If we put these three items together, it would reach 26.7% (World Economic Handbook, CASS, 1981). Correspondently, in Chinese urban regions, we had 1.5% for rent, 0.61% for medical care and 0.59% for education by the end of 1982, and the sum of three items was only 2.7% (*China Statistical Yearbook*, 1983).

Because of this small proportion of expenses in China, the corresponding Chinese Engels' Coefficient during that period was oscillating around 60%, 58.6% in 1982, 57.5,

56.9 and 56.7 for 1978, '80 and '81, respectively, and 59.2 and 58.0% for 1983 and 1984, respectively. However, the Engels' Coefficient in the US was 37.7, 37.6 and 40.0% for 1978, '79 and '80, respectively.

The fact that China was at a low stage of development with a high proportion of food consumption against the US at a high stage of development with a low proportion of food consumption cannot explain this huge difference: Approximately 60% for China and 40% for the US.

It is only by considering other factors that we can better understand this gap. Chinese consumers have a lower weight compared with American consumers in the above expenses, and it is because the Chinese government allocated a large amount of subsidies to public housing. For example, housing subsidies in China reached around 20 billion RMB in 1981, which represents approximately 25% of total national wages (82 billion RMB). The proportion of rent consumption occupied about 20% of total expenses in China that year. This proportion is not lower than in the US, and we can also find similar results in medical care and education.

What was the reasonable RIR for China during that period? We can find several answers: One can argue that a good RIR is, on average, 11% for the middle-income states and 15% for developed ones (Tian J. G., 2010); another one says that if a state has its Engel's Coefficient between 40% and 50%, its reasonable RIR shall be between 12% to 19%[3].

China had its Engel's Coefficient of 53% for urban households in 1992 and slightly over 50% for the next three years (53.0%, 50.3%, 50.0% and 50.1% for 1992, '93, '94 and '95, respectively). The trend drops to 36.2%

---

3 Source: http://www.51Labour.com/ China Labour Consultation Website.

in 2012 after hitting 38.2% in 2001. (See the above table for details)

No matter what kind of method we use, the results will be approximately the same: 11-12% in RIR for China would be considered good. Nevertheless, as just mentioned, it was only 0.73% in 1992, that is to say, that 14 years after the launch of the economic reform, China was completely distorted in terms of RIR. This total distortion in RIR reflected the urgent need for housing reform in China.

Consequently, state investment in housing was virtually non-recoverable (Tang G. 1989). As a result, the problem of heavy government financial burdens (Wang Y. P. & A. Murie, 1996) became more and more acute. How to fund housing, not only in the building of new apartments but also in the management and maintenance of existing housing was one of the puzzles haunting Chinese officials and leaders of *Danwei*.

The accommodation conditions were also execrable. From the following figure, we can easily find that the progress in the average flat area (m2) per capita during around 30 years since the establishment of the New Republic till the start of economic reform was minuscule in absolute terms, with only 2.2 m2 from 4.5 m2 in 1950 to 6.7 m2 in 1978. However, it had a huge percentage value (48.89%). *"Dwelling Narrowness" (Woju,* or *Snail Dwelling* if translated literally), the title of a popular TV series in 2009 in China, illustrates this sort of dwelling conditions in China mostly before the housing reform, and even today in mega cities like Shanghai.

Dilapidated Neighborhoods is another example of how bad conditions were in terms of housing in those areas. They are the old structures like *Siheyuan* in Beijing and *Shikumen* in Shanghai, and most of them were also public housing distributed to *Danwei* employees, except for a small part of these *Dilapidated Houses* held by "indigenous" inhabitants who inherited their properties from their ancestors. Luckily, their properties were not confiscated at the beginning of the New Republic. Zhang H. (2009) argued: "Due to the long stagnation in housing construction during the first 30 years of the People's Republic of China, those structures were in chaos in terms of facility quality and management and regarded as uninhabitable, suffering from over-crowdedness and a lack of proper maintenance".

Figure 14: Evolution of Average Floor Area per Capita in China (sq. m.)

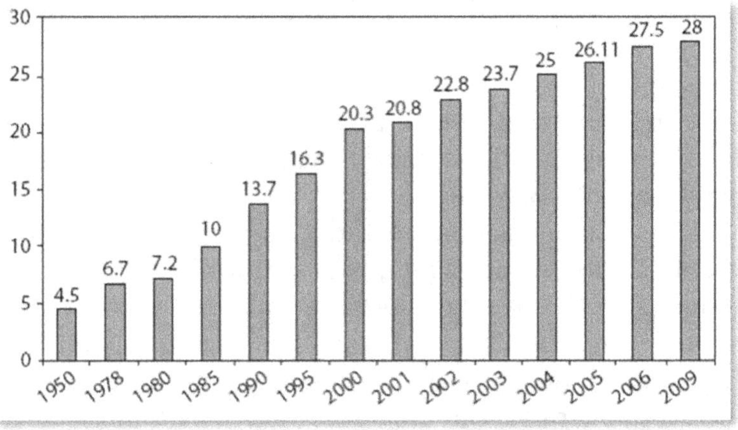

Source: Ministry of Housing and Urban-Rural Development (2009)

Tongzilou (*"Tube-Shaped Apartment"* translated literally), *is* another type of run-down house, like a dormitory without a private kitchen and bathroom akin to a military camp but with several floors. The majority of *Tongzilou* were inside university campuses and some *Danwei*. These old structures were built under Soviet influence when the U.S.S.R. were still China's "Old Big Brother" during the 1950s and 1960s. Together with the *Dilapidated Neighborhoods, Tongzilou* had neither private toilets nor independent kitchens and were therefore called *"non-apartment houses"*.

In addition, other problems were getting increasingly severe, such as the problem of unfair distribution wherein privileged households manipulated the allocation system (Chiu R. L. H., 1996). There was also the problem of urban zoning issues and of corruption in the process of distribution and allocation (Wang Y. P. & A. Murie, 2000 & 1996 respectively). More and more extreme cases took place during *Danwei*'s housing distribution, even leading to riots.

The purely planned system can work relatively well only under certain circumstances, but cannot be sustained in the long run. So was the Chinese planned welfare-oriented housing distribution system. Housing was distributed by the state or *Danwei*, the rent for public housing was low and kept on getting lower since 1958 to the extent that the rent was unable to fund the housing anymore. The government's financial capacity and the financial situation of *Danwei* were insufficient, and the construction of new housing and maintenance of old structures could not be ensured, while the accommodations could not be improved. A housing vicious circle in China before the reform prevailed. In short, this socialist or socialistic distribution system of housing could not work anymore.

2. Reform Schedule

Previous literature shows different methods of classification in 30 years of China's housing reform, such as two phases, three phases and four phases. I consider it more logical to classify those 30 years into six phases with four benchmarks.

1) Six Phases

In this paper, different stages of housing reform from 1980 to the present are summarized into six phases as follows:

Phase 1 Pilot Trial Phase, 1980-1988 (8 years)

One characteristic of Chinese reform is to experiment before officially launching it, so this pilot trial phase lasted 8 years. This demonstrates the prudent attitude of the Chinese government towards this totally new phenomenon in the New China's history.

The final goal of housing reform was to realize commercialization and socialization in China's housing reform. Three sub-reforms explored the feasibility of selling public housing, including the old and newly-built ones, of commercializing the housing and of reforming the rent system. It was also in this stage that China started to draft the housing law.

Phase 2 Step-by-Step Boost Phase, 1988-1994 (6 years)

The State Council decided in February 1988 to use 3-5 years to boost housing reform in stages in urban areas across China, and decided In November 1991 to boost nationwide housing reform. In this phase, the mission of housing reform was to reasonably modify public housing rent. One of the measures taken was to sell to individual residents both old and new public housing.

From the end of the 1980s to the start of the 1990s, Chinese urban inhabitants started to loan from banks to buy houses. It was the very first time in the New China's history.

Phase 3 Deepening Phase, 1994-1998 (4 years)

The Decision on the Deepening of Urban Housing System Reform (Guofa 199443) was promulgated by the State Council of the People's Republic of China in July 1994. This advanced for the first time the housing supply system based on the government-subsidized affordable housing aimed at low- and middle-income families, and the housing supply system based on the commodity houses was aimed at the high-income families. The "Three-Level Pattern" started to form in the Chinese housing market.

The decision boosted for the first time the nationwide Public Housing Accumulation Fund. This fund was inspired by the Mandatory Provident Fund (MPF) in Singapore.

The decision advanced the reinforcement of efforts in the building of affordable housing to solve the accommodation problem for low- and middle-income families and started to implement the Anju Project (a form of government-subsidized housing) in 1995. In short, selling homes to the low- and middle-income families at the "cost price (CP)". The government started to sell public housing at market price to high-income families. It also stipulated for the first time strict controls over the development of high-end real estate projects.

The decision also encouraged joint venture housing construction and the development of housing cooperatives to accelerate the urban redevelopment in the areas of dilapidated neighborhoods. Finally, it also reinforced rent reform and started to adopt preferential policies, like reductions or remissions, or subsidies for low-income families.

Phase 4 Monetization-Starting Phase, 1998-2003 (5 years)

The Resolutions on Continuing Urban Housing System Reform, Accelerating Housing Development (Guofa 199823) was promulgated by the State Council in July 1998. These resolutions terminated the material housing distribution since the second half of 1998 and started to gradually adopt the monetary distribution[4], a kind of new monetary compensation system to replace the traditional welfare housing system. These "Resolutions" advanced for the first time the establishment and perfection of the multi-layer urban housing supply system based mainly on affordable housing. It also stipulated for the first time the restructuring of investment in housing, especially in the development of affordable housing (Anju Project).

The resolutions also stated for the first time that all commercial banks would be able to grant personal housing loans in all urban areas, and advanced for the first time the establishment of a real estate management mechanism. This mechanism was socialized, specialized and market-based.

The resolutions likewise provided for stabilizing affordable housing prices, the regulation of real estate prices, continue to develop joint venture housing development and by cooperatives to accelerate the construction of affordable housing. Since the second half of 1998, they started to sell existing public housing primarily at cost-price, and tried to link this with the prices of affordable housing.

---

[4] The Monetary Distribution: the 'welfare housing' was distributed 'in kind' before 1998; after 1998 reform, real housing is not distributed any more to employees who will be paid 'in currency' instead; in other words, welfare housing system was replaced by monetary compensation system.

For rent of low-price public housing provided by the government or *Danwei* to the lowest-income families, pricing was to be made by the government; and for commodity housing bought or rented by high-income families, the market was to regulate pricing. It was also stated that the real estate developer could fix the sale or rent price according to the cost and demand, and that the government should place a cap on the developer's revenue.

Finally, the "resolutions" reinforced the management of land prices, established the regular announcement system for the standard land price, and continued to boost the rent reform.

Phase 5 Security-Establishing Phase, 2003-2007 (4 years)

In this phase, the main goal was to regulate the housing price, and to establish the housing security system. The State Council has successively promulgated a series of important documents such as the Former Guo[5] 8 Articles, Latter Guo 8 Articles and Guo 6 Articles to maintain the relative stability of housing prices, especially those of ordinary commodity housing and affordable housing, and to establish and perfect the housing security system which suits China's specific situation.

In terms of housing price stability, these Documents increased the housing supply by controlling demand to stabilize housing prices by loosening the conflicts between supply and demand. In terms of the establishment of the housing security system, they reinforced the government mission in housing security, accelerated the building of low-rent housing in urban areas, regulated the

---

[5] Guo: idem with 'Guofa', abbreviation of 'Decision or directive promulgated by Chinese State Council'.

development of affordable housing, developed the secondary housing market and housing rent market to solve the housing difficulties of low-income families.

Phase 6 Security-Reinforcing Phase, 2007-

Since 2007, we entered the phase of reinforcing housing security. The low-rent housing system lagged behind in urban areas, the affordable housing system was far from being perfect, the concerned matching policies has not been established, and some low-income families still suffered from acute housing problems.

In August 2007, the State Council promulgated "The Several Opinions of the State Council on Solving the Housing Difficulties of Urban Low-Income Families" (No.24 [2007]). These "Opinions" put at an unprecedented level the "Security Housing", another milestone in China's housing reform history.

2) Four Benchmarks

China's housing reform the essential benchmarks were as follows:

Table 4: Four Benchmarks of Housing Reform in China

Benchmark 1 **1980's Speech**	The economic reform started in 1978. Two years later, Deng xiaoping made an important speech on April 2, 1980 concerning the housing problem. This speech has been generally considered as the commencement of China's housing reform. He dealt with the position of the construction sector and policies on housing. Deng designed the whole process of the housing sector, including housing construction, transactions, distribution and consumption. Deng put forward the sales of public housing and adjustment of rent in advocating the purchase of housing by individuals.
Benchmark 2 **1994's "Decision"**	In July 1994, the State Council promulgated its "Decision on the Deepening of Urban Housing System Reform". The Decision was to set throughout the country major reform guidelines of "housing's socialization and commercialization", to establish the Public Housing Accumulation Fund, to sell at production cost the public housing and to start the Anju Project.
Benchmark 3 **1998's "Resolutions"**	In July 1998, the State Council adjusted the housing policy and issued "The Resolutions on Continuing Urban Housing System Reform, Accelerating Housing Development". Its significance was to terminate the welfare housing distribution, to establish a housing distribution based on the market, and to advance the development of the housing sector as one pillar of the economy. After that, the traditional material housing distribution was replaced by the monetary distribution at the end of 1998.
Benchmark 4 **2007's "Opinions"**	On 13th August 2007, "The Several Opinions of the State Council on Solving the Housing Difficulties of Urban Low-Income Families" (No.24 [2007] of the State Council) was promulgated. These "Opinions" were completed through the segmentation in the framework of government-subsidized housing, the dual model of "Policy + Market" in avoiding over-emphasis on single market rail model.

3. Urban Redevelopment: A Special Housing Reform

As a special form of housing reform in China, the "Urban Redevelopment", originally "Urban Renewal", was something that each industrializing state had to meet.

This problem was acute for the US as the 19th century slum housing consisted of buildings with warrens of tiny, poorly ventilated rooms that resulted in a high incidence of infant mortality and infectious diseases among the European immigrant population.

Then, reforms began at the beginning of the 20th century with the New York State Tenement House Law and continued in the 1930s with zoning ordinances. Federal loans funded the building of housing for workers. The major period of urban renovation in the US began with Title I of the 1949 Housing Act. The Urban Renewal Program provided for wholesale demolition of slums and the construction of some 800,000 properties throughout the nation. The program's goals included eliminating substandard housing, constructing adequate housing, reducing *de facto* segregation, and revitalizing city economies[6].

China started to deal with its problem of Urban Redevelopment in the 1980s, no sooner after the start of the economic reform. As mentioned in this paper, the old structures like *Siheyuan* in Beijing and *Shikumen* in Shanghai were, in most cases, public housing of *Danwei*. After 30 years of the socialistic system, Zhang H. (2009) said those structures were in chaos in terms of facility quality and management, and regarded as uninhabitable, suffering from over-crowdedness and a lack of proper maintenance.

Let's look at the urbanization movement in China of which the spark was the reform and opening-up policy, where urbanization was the true stimulus of the urban redevelopment.

Population growth is an important factor, especially with economic growth stimulated by the reform and opening up, and the population grew in urban areas despite China's strict Family Planning Policy.

---

[6] Source: The US History Encyclopedia.

Demographic mobility is also a crucial factor in China's industrialization. If we consider population growth a static factor, demographic mobility is a dynamic one. These two variables influenced the urbanization process and housing reform in China, and vice versa.

1) Population Growth

The NBSC announced on September 17, 2009 that the total population living in the cities at prefecture level and above (counties excluded) was, by the end of 2008, over 370 million, 8.5-fold higher than that in 1949.

Figure 15: Population and Its Composition in China 1978-2008

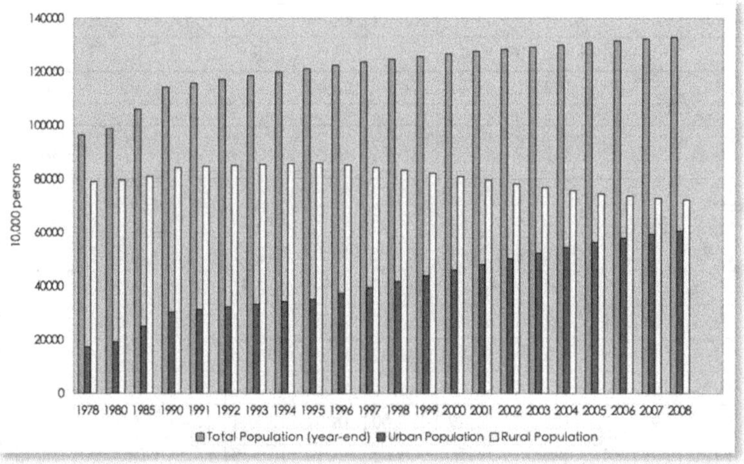

Source: China Statistical Yearbook 2009

Refer to the following table for details about the population and its composition in China between 1978 and 2008, and between 1949 and 2012.

Despite the Family Planning policy which was generally considered as the most severe policy of population control in the world and criticized by Western states, China's total population was still huge in absolute terms. Including counties, the total urban population reached 606.67 million in 2008 against only 172.45 million in 1978 (NBSC, 2009)—in other words, over 3.52-fold higher than in 1978 in urban areas, while the total population was only 1.38-fold higher. The population growth in urban areas was 2.55-fold higher than the total population.

Table 5: Population and Its Composition in China 1949-2012 (Population Unit: 1,000,000 persons)

Year	Total			By Sex				By Residence	
	Population	Male		Female		Urban		Rural	
	(year-end)	Pop.	Prop.	Pop.	Prop.	Pop.	Prop.	Pop.	Prop.
1949	541.67	281.45	51.96	260.22	48.04	57.65	10.64	484.02	89.36
1950	551.96	286.69	51.94	265.27	48.06	61.69	11.18	490.27	88.82
1951	563.00	292.31	51.92	270.69	48.08	66.32	11.78	496.68	88.22
1955	614.65	318.09	51.75	296.56	48.25	82.85	13.48	531.80	86.52
1960	662.07	342.83	51.78	319.24	48.22	130.73	19.75	531.34	80.25
1965	725.38	371.28	51.18	354.10	48.82	130.45	17.98	594.93	82.02
1970	829.92	426.86	51.43	403.06	48.57	144.24	17.38	685.68	82.62
1971	852.29	438.19	51.41	414.10	48.59	147.11	17.26	705.18	82.74
1972	871.77	448.13	51.40	423.64	48.60	149.35	17.13	722.42	82.87
1973	892.11	458.76	51.42	433.35	48.58	153.45	17.20	738.66	82.80
1974	908.59	467.27	51.43	441.32	48.57	155.95	17.16	752.64	82.84
1975	924.20	475.64	51.47	448.56	48.53	160.30	17.34	763.90	82.66
1976	937.17	482.57	51.49	454.60	48.51	163.41	17.44	773.76	82.56
1977	949.74	489.08	51.50	460.66	48.50	166.69	17.55	783.05	82.45
1978	962.59	495.67	51.49	466.92	48.51	172.45	17.92	790.14	82.08
1979	975.42	501.92	51.46	473.50	48.54	184.95	18.96	790.47	81.04
1980	987.05	507.85	51.45	479.20	48.55	191.40	19.39	795.65	80.61
1981	1,000.72	515.19	51.48	485.53	48.52	201.71	20.16	799.01	79.84
1982	1,016.54	523.52	51.50	493.02	48.50	214.80	21.13	801.74	78.87
1983	1,030.08	531.52	51.60	498.56	48.40	222.74	21.62	807.34	78.38
1984	1,043.57	538.48	51.60	505.09	48.40	240.17	23.01	803.40	76.99
1985	1,058.51	547.25	51.70	511.26	48.30	250.94	23.71	807.57	76.29
1986	1,075.07	555.81	51.70	519.26	48.30	263.66	24.52	811.41	75.48
1987	1,093.00	562.90	51.50	530.10	48.50	276.74	25.32	816.26	74.68

1988	1,110.26	572.01	51.52	538.25	48.48	286.61	25.81	823.65	74.19
1989	1,127.04	580.99	51.55	546.05	48.45	295.40	26.21	831.64	73.79
1990	1,143.33	589.04	51.52	554.29	48.48	301.95	26.41	841.38	73.59
1991	1,158.23	594.66	51.34	563.57	48.66	312.03	26.94	846.20	73.06
1992	1,171.71	598.11	51.05	573.60	48.95	321.75	27.46	849.96	72.54
1993	1,185.17	604.72	51.02	580.45	48.98	331.73	27.99	853.44	72.01
1994	1,198.50	612.46	51.10	586.04	48.90	341.69	28.51	856.81	71.49
1995	1,211.21	618.08	51.03	593.13	48.97	351.74	29.04	859.47	70.96
1996	1,223.89	622.00	50.82	601.89	49.18	373.04	30.48	850.85	69.52
1997	1,236.26	631.31	51.07	604.95	48.93	394.49	31.91	841.77	68.09
1998	1,247.61	639.40	51.25	608.21	48.75	416.08	33.35	831.53	66.65
1999	1,257.86	646.92	51.43	610.94	48.57	437.48	34.78	820.38	65.22
2000	1,267.43	654.37	51.63	613.06	48.37	459.06	36.22	808.37	63.78
2001	1,276.27	656.72	51.46	619.55	48.54	480.64	37.66	795.63	62.34
2002	1,284.53	661.15	51.47	623.38	48.53	502.12	39.09	782.41	60.91
2003	129227	665.56	51.50	626.71	48.50	523.76	40.53	768.51	59.47
2004	1,299.88	669.76	51.52	630.12	48.48	542.83	41.76	757.05	58.24
2005	1,307.56	673.75	51.53	633.81	48.47	562.12	42.99	745.44	57.01
2006	1,314.48	677.28	51.52	637.20	48.48	582.88	44.34	731.60	55.66
2007	1,321.29	680.48	51.50	640.81	48.50	606.33	45.89	714.96	54.11
2008	1,328.02	683.57	51.47	644.45	48.53	624.03	46.99	703.99	53.01
2009	1,334.50	686.47	51.44	648.03	48.56	645.12	48.34	689.38	51.66
2010	1,340.91	687.48	51.27	653.43	48.73	669.78	49.95	671.13	50.05
2011	1,347.35	690.68	51.26	656.67	48.74	690.79	51.27	656.56	48.73
2012	1,354.04	693.95	51.25	660.09	48.75	711.82	52.57	642.22	47.43

a) Figures 1981 (inclusive) are from household registrations. The years 1982, 1990, 2000 and 2010 are the census year estimates. The rest of the data covered in those tables have been estimated on the basis of the annual national sample surveys of population. The same applies to the relevant succeeding tables.

b) Total population and population by sex include military personnel of the Chinese People's Liberation Army. Military personnel are classified as urban population in the item of population by residence.

Source: Table 3-1, China Statistical Yearbook 2013

The population size was already influential in the urban redevelopment during the urbanization process, but the demographic mobility was more influential, especially for a country like China.

2) Demographic Mobility

Concerning the data announced by the NBSC, they were higher than those given by the Urbanization Commission. I cited four examples in the following table:

Table 6: Urban Population Share in China by Two Institutions

Year	Source: National Bureau of Statistics of China	Source: China International Urbanization Development Strategy Research Commission	Difference between NBSC & Commission
	Proportion of Urban Population (%)	Proportion of Urban Population (%)	(%)
1999	34.78	25.51	9.27
2000	36.22	26.08	10.14
2006	43.90	32.53	11.37
2007	44.94	32.93	12.01
Average	39.96	29.26	10.70

Source: Calculation based on the data given by the survey report of the "Urbanization Commission" and data from the National Bureau of Statistics of China

The difference between the two institutions is large - at 10.7 percentage points on average - as the average for these four years was around only 40% and 30%, respectively. When the Bureau of Statistics used its method from 2006 based on the classification by residence in urban areas (for the residents with *hukou* and those without *hukou*, but dwelling for a period of over six months) or rural areas, the Urbanization Commission insisted on using the non-agricultural population as the numerator. According to this commission, the numerator is "an important indicator and relatively more complete and systemic to evaluate China's urbanization level" (Survey report of the Urbanization Commission, 2008 and 2009).

The non-agricultural population is those with *hukou* in China. The parentheses are not meant to compare the two methods. On the contrary they demonstrate China's high demographic mobility. As we have just discussed, the gap between the data of the Bureau of Statistics and the Urbanization Commission was mainly due to this specific population segment who were agricultural inhabitants but moved to urban areas and dwelled there for a period of over six months (accepted by the Bureau of Statistics in its data) without being able to acquire a *hukou* (still omitted by the Urbanization Commission in its data).

The importance of the 10.7 average percentage points justifies the importance of mobility in China, and the upward trend from 1999 to 2007 shows the increase of this demographic mobility while the accelerating trend from 9.27 to 12.01 percentage points demonstrates the importance of this mobility.

This high demographic mobility was among the factors which fueled the housing reform. We will deal with the urban redevelopment later, and also with skyrocketing housing prices.

3) Urbanization Process

China was experiencing rapid urbanization, but in order to have a complete understanding, let's look first at its urbanization process since the foundation of the New Republic in 1949 to 2007 as depicted in the following chart:

Figure 16: Urbanization Rate in China, 1949-2007

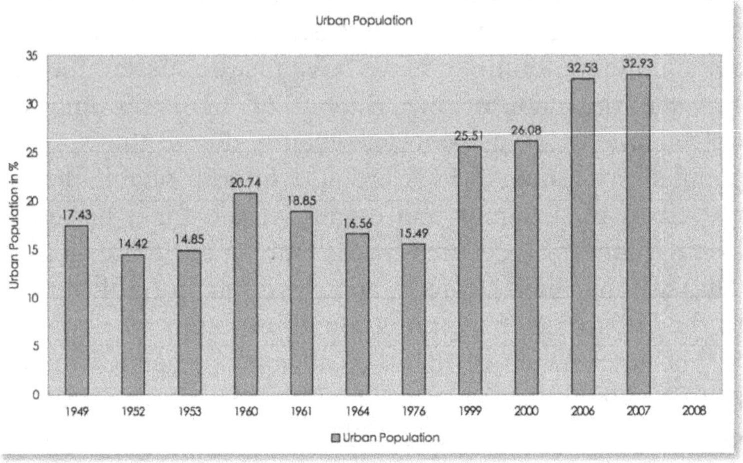

Sources: Survey report on China's Urbanization Rate, versions 2008 and 2009, by China International Urbanization Development Strategy Research Commission

China International Urbanization Development Strategy Research Commission revealed the data on December 6, 2008 in its Survey report on China's Urbanization Rate (2008 and 2009 versions). This report was considered as a complete and systemic research on China's urbanization rate from 1949 to 2007 and 2008, respectively. According to this report, China's urbanization process can be classified into four stages:

Stage I: Pre-Cultural Revolution Stage

This stage was characterized by slow development from 1949 to 1964. China experienced several ups and downs. Between 1949 and 1952, the urbanization rate dropped by one percentage point each year from 17.43% to 14.42%. Between 1953 and 1960, the rate increased by around six percentage points from 14.85% to 20.74%. And between 1961 and 1964, the rate declined from 18.85% to 16.56%.

Stage II: Cultural Revolution Stage

This stage was characterized by stagnant development from 1965 to 1975. China's urbanization stagnated because of the Cultural Revolution, dropping 1.26 percentage points within ten years.

Stage III: Post-Cultural Revolution Stage

Unlike the previous stage, development in this stage was stable from 1976 to 1999. China urbanized consistently from 15.49% in 1976 to 25.51% in 1999, or an increase of around 10 percentage points.

Stage IV

The years from 2000 to 2006 showed rapid development (according to 2006 according to the 2008 version, or to 2007 based on the 2009 version). China accelerated its urbanization process, with growth rising from 26.08% to 32.53% and to 32.93% (until 2006 and 2007, respectively) by around seven percentage points in seven years.

The above data given by the Urbanization Commission was more or less conservative. The National Bureau of Statistics of China (NBSC) had its own data, as follows:

Figure 17: Urban and Rural Population Share in China, 1978-2008

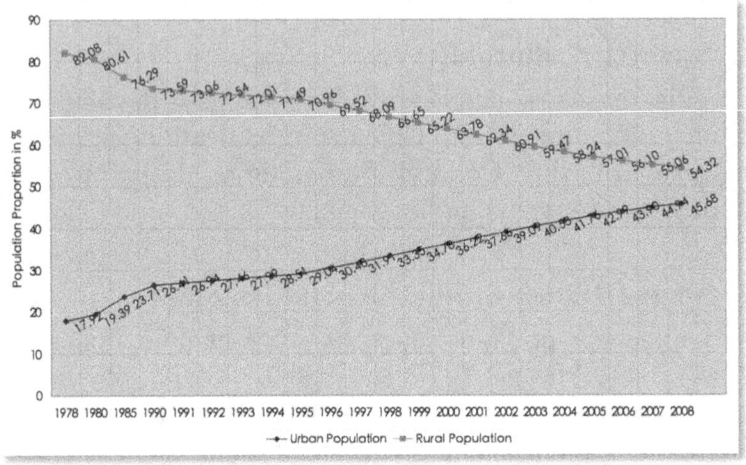

Source: China Statistical Yearbook 2009

The NBSC announced on September 17, 2009 in a series of reports on New China's 60 Years of Achievements that by the end of 2008, the urbanization rate in China had reached 45.68%, 19 percentage points higher than in 1991, with the rate in 1978 only 17.92%.

The share in percentage is indicated in the figure above. The convergence trend was obvious: The blue line representing the share of the urban population rose from 17.92% in 1978 to 45.68% in 2008, while the rose-colored line representing the rural population declined from 82.08% to 54.32% in 2008.

During the urbanization process, the most important factor was the population growth and demographic mobility. It is truer in China, and the demographic variables were more influential in China than in other countries due to the size of China's population (around 1.37 billion by the end of 2012 based on NBSC data) and the extremely low level of urbanization (17.92% in 1978, China Statistical Yearbook 2009).

Stage V: 2011-present

We depict the composition using data from the China Statistical Yearbook 2013. The horizontal ordinate uses 10 years as the time interval for uniformity.

From the previous table and the following figure, we find that the convergence point is between 2010 and 2011: 49.95% for the urban population and 50.05% for the rural one in 2010, and 51.27% for the urban population and 48.73 for the rural one in 2011.

It was the first time in the history of New China that urbanization surpassed 50%. By 2012, the urban population stood at 52.57 percentage points.

Figure 18: Urban and Rural Population Share in China, 1949-2012

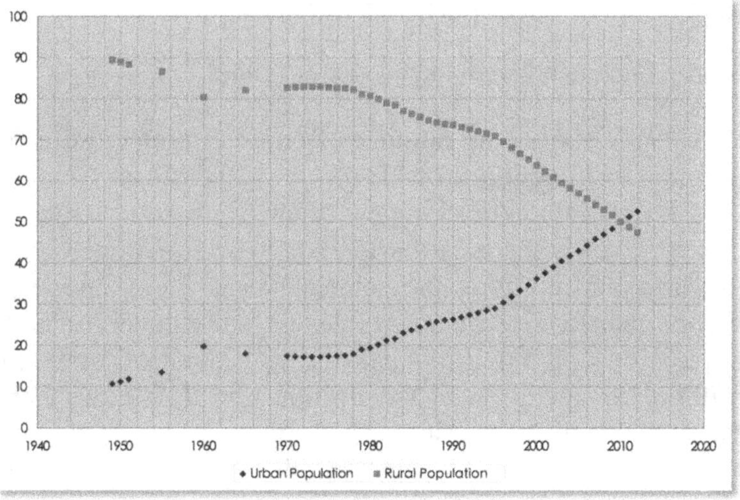

Source: China Statistical Yearbook 2013

With the population expansion and demographic mobility, urbanization grew even faster, with cities sprouting like mushrooms, and their numbers multiplying.

4) Number of Cities

The total number of cities in China had reached 655 (in which 287 were at least at the prefecture level), 176 more than in 1991. In other words, 11 cities were created annually from 1991 to 2008 and 2012 on average (NBSC, September 17, 2009, and 2012).

Table 7: Number of Cities at Prefecture Level and Higher in China, 2008 and 2012

	(unit)						
Year	Total	Grouped by Population in Urban Districts					
		4 million and over	2 - 4 million	1 - 2 million	0.5 - 1 million	0.2 - 0.5 million	under 0.2 million
2008	287	13	28	81	110	51	4
2012	289	14	31	82	108	50	4

Source: China Statistical Yearbook 2009 and 2013

Table 7 shows the number of cities at prefecture level and higher in China up to 2008. A prefecture in China is an administrative level higher than a county. A city at county level is the most basic and smallest administrative division, and a city at prefecture level is a city one level higher than a city at county level. Thirteen cities have populations of 4 million and above, 28 cities from 2-4 million, 81 cities have 1-2 million and 110 cities have 500,000-1 million people.

The 13 cities with over 4 million inhabitants and 28 cities of 2-4 million suffer the classic mega city and big city housing problem, while the 191 cities with from 500,000-2 million faced a housing problem as those which have been newly transformed from small towns or previous big villages do, and this sort of transformation represented a challenge to policy-makers of these cities.

In 2012, an additional city had over 4 million people over 2008, 3 cities with 2-4 million people, and one city more with 1-2 million more people. As such, there were two less cities with a population of 500,000-1 million compared to 2008 and one city less with a population of from 200,000-500,000 million. The number of cities with a population of under 200,000 remained at four.

5) Urban Construction

With regard to urban construction, refer to the annex which depicts city construction by region until 2008 and 2012. I have kept only one part of the data just to illustrate the scale of urban construction, the disproportion between the area of built districts and the urban areas, and the population density of urban areas. All these represent the characteristics of urbanization in China.

Table 8: City Construction by Region in China 2008

Region	Urban Area (sq. km)	Area of Built Districts (sq. km)	Area of Land Used for Urban Constructio n (sq. km)	Land Put in Requisition for State Constructio n Projects (sq. km)	Populatio n Density of Urban Area (persons/ sq. km)
National Total	178110.3	36295.3	39140.5	1344.6	2080
Beijing	12187.0	1310.9	1310.9		1181
Tianjin	2236.1	640.9	640.9	70.3	2858
Shanghai	6340.5		2429.1		2978
Jiangsu	12250.8	2904.3	2991.7	107.1	1905
Zhejiang	10011.1	1939.1	2025.1	102.1	1757
Shandong	18690.4	3261.0	3191.5	93.9	1413
Guangdong	18485.8	4132.6	3943.1	37.8	2370
Guangxi	5719.3	840.6	1006.1	40.5	1461

Chongqing	5590.6	708.4	694.1	56.0	1574
Sichuan	5480.8	1391.7	1382.2	64.5	2677
Tibet	295.0	79.0	79.0		1557
Xinjiang	1183.2	751.0	783.4	6.7	4987

Source: National Bureau of Statistics of China, 2009; For brevity, only 12 representative regions have been selected.

As shown in Table 8, the urban area for Beijing is 12,187 km2, and the area of land used for urban construction and the area of built districts until 2008 was 1,310.9 km2, which represented only around 11% of the urban area. 1,310.9 km2 means a square with a side length of 36.2 kilometers corresponds to the length of 40 *li* of Chang'an Avenue (20 km for the classical Chang'an main body) plus the extension part of less than 20 km. The density of urban area in Table 8 (1,181 persons/km2 in Beijing) was calculated on the basis of the whole urban area. Therefore, most of the population was still concentrated in the area of built districts in "Small Beijing".

Tianjin and Shanghai shall also surprise us by their high population density of 2,858 and 2,978 persons/km2, respectively. The ratio of land used for urban construction/urban area in Shanghai was high at 38.3%. This can be explained by its specific geographic conditions and non-extensibility of its land. This high ratio illustrates the extreme population density of Shanghai.

Please see the following table for data which includes 2012.

Table 9: City Construction by Region in China in 2012

12-4 Statistics on City Construction by Region (2012)					
Region	Urban Area (sq.km)	Area of Built Districts (sq.km)	Area of Land Used for Urban Construction (sq.km)	Land Put in Requisition for State Construction Projects (sq.km)	Population Density of Urban Area (persons/ sq.km)
National Total	183039.4	45565.8	45750.7	2161.5	2307
Beijing	12187.0	1261.1	1445.0	42.2	1464
Tianjin	2334.5	722.1	722.1	55.7	2782
Hebei	6611.2	1738.9	1609.3	19.7	2411
Shanxi	3427.2	1013.8	944.1	26.8	3028
Inner Mongolia	8501.0	1132.8	1198.8	17.9	1032
Liaoning	13966.5	2329.1	2261.3	194.8	1624
Jilin	3956.6	1293.8	1209.8	56.0	2878
Heilongjiang	2718.3	1725.5	1747.7	39.7	5054
Shanghai	6340.5	998.8	2904.3	42.0	3754
Jiangsu	13957.0	3655.1	3701.9	245.9	2002
Zhejiang	10515.2	2296.3	2246.7	115.2	1786
Anhui	5569.1	1696.0	1682.0	128.6	2401
Fujian	4500.9	1203.1	1126.1	72.5	2388
Jiangxi	1949.6	1077.6	1034.3	65.9	4663
Shandong	21421.5	3927.0	3854.4	150.7	1349
Henan	4628.0	2219.1	2083.4	44.7	4964
Hubei	9052.3	1889.6	2126.7	34.3	2004
Hunan	4623.5	1465.1	1430.2	69.1	3030
Guangdong	15984.1	5026.4	4083.4	286.3	2927
Guangxi	6067.4	1083.6	1029.8	88.9	1528
Hainan	1149.1	265.6	253.4	11.2	2079
Chongqing	6105.7	1051.7	859.5	75.3	1832
Sichuan	6205.0	1901.7	1855.6	71.1	2866
Guizhou	1816.6	586.1	555.5	17.1	3324
Yunnan	2143.8	859.9	846.6	62.5	4029
Tibet	337.0	119.7	111.0		1655
Shaanxi	1504.4	863.5	776.2	28.7	5483
Gansu	1292.4	681.6	642.7	52.9	4369
Qinghai	512.3	122.1	122.0	2.9	2674
Ningxia	2103.2	399.6	332.9	10.7	1251
Xinjiang	1558.5	959.6	954.1	32.4	4312

Source: National Bureau of Statistics of China, 2013

We have just discussed the urbanization process in China with its four stages, the population expansion despite the family planning policy implemented by the government, the high demographic mobility based on different statistical methods that the two most reliable official institutions used, the increase in the number of cities, and urban construction showing the high urban density in China.

According to the Bluebook (April 14, 2010) of the Chinese Academy of Social Sciences, China was in the accelerating urbanization phase at an annual growth rate of around 1.09%.

Zhang has tried to explain why the urban redevelopment in China in the past ten years seemed more sustainable than the slum clearances in the US in the 1950s and 1960s, despite the identical approach of demolition of dilapidated neighborhoods. Housing reform in China should be seen as a unique institutional phenomenon based on his research.

The final solution to abandoning those dilapidated neighborhoods and enabling the residents to find dwellings elsewhere by using their monetary relocation compensation *(*Zhang H., 2009*)* is not always a good solution. We do not want to ignore the fact that this was one of the ways taken by some local governments towards certain areas of neighborhoods. However, in most cases, a combination of different methods or a portfolio of policies had to be adopted during this complex process of urban redevelopment in China.

SECTION 2 FINANCE AND REAL ESTATE

In Section 1 we discussed the real estate reforms which were one part of the reforms adopted by the Chinese government during the last three decades.

The relationship between finance and real estate is tight in China. Before analyzing this relationship, let's look first look at the multiple "fuels" of the housing market expansion in China.

1. "Fuels" of Housing Market Expansion

It is well known that the Chinese housing market "exploded" with the deepening of real restate reforms. We will try to determine what the original impetus was in this housing market expansion, and what the "fuels" were for such a surge despite the global financial crisis, while normally leads to a slump in prices, such as in the US and Dubai during the sub-prime crisis, and in most Asian countries in the Asian financial crisis. It can be more complex due to the effect of asset substitution under the crisis.

The following figure shows the average selling price of commercial buildings by year in China from 1991 to 2012. We will focus on the watershed year of 1997 because it was the last year of the old welfare-based housing distribution system. With the Benchmark 3, 1998's Resolutions, the housing market started to develop.

Figure 19: Yearly Average Selling Price of Commercialized Buildings, 1991-2012

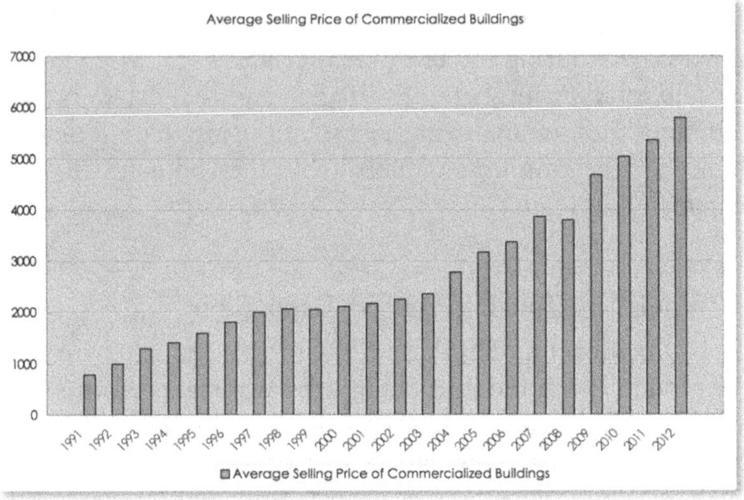

Source: China Statistical Yearbook 2005 & 2013

Figure 19 shows the evolution of housing prices, at first slowly but surely. From around 2,000 RMB/m2 from 1997 to 1999, the slap flattened out from 2000 to 2003. But since 2004, there was an accelerated increase until 2007. We previously discussed 2007 in Benchmark 4: 2007's Opinions on the eve of the global financial crisis.

2008 is a rare time in which housing price declined. Though the decrease was slight at only 64 RMB/m2 from 3,864 RMB/m2 to 3,800 RMB/m2, it represented the influence of the financial crisis on China. Prices quickly rose in 2009 to 4,861 RMB/m2, 27.92% higher than the previous year. This upward trend prevailed until 2012.

To better understand this, we will begin by discussing different stimuli, such as specific Chinese culture of land, economic/GDP growth, disposable income growth and savings growth, and the financial growth for the housing market's expansion.

1) Culture of Land in China

Land was their first priority. In traditional China, especially during unstable periods like wars and changes in dynasty, land and housing were the most convenient way to preserve value, even ahead of precious metals like silver and gold were susceptible to theft. Land and housing were also the symbols of the fortune one held, and this translated to social status.

Modern Chinese society has since evolved, but this "Culture of Land" remains rooted in Chinese people. As China has become an urbanizing state, from an urbanization rate of 20% in 1978 to 45.68% in 2008 (based on the announcement of the National Bureau of Statistics of China) and 46.6% in 2009 (according to the March 29, 2010 announcement of the State Council), a great number of rural inhabitants were becoming urban inhabitants, with or without *hukou*, due to the unprecedented migration generated by the rapid urbanization in China.

According to Article 2 of The Law of Land Administration of the People's Republic of China *(amended on August 29, 1998)*, "The People's Republic of China resorts to a socialist public ownership, i.e. an ownership by the whole people and ownership by cooperatives, of land. In ownership by the whole people, the State Council is empowered to be on behalf of the State to administer the land owned by the State. Land use rights may be transferred by law."

Therefore, under the actual socialist regime, inhabitants can only possess land use rights. But this lasted no more than 70 years for residential property and 40 years for commercial property according to the "Interim Regulations of the People's Republic of China Concerning the Assignment and Transfer of the Right to the Use of the State-owned Land in the Urban Areas"

(May 19th 1990, State Council). Housing has become the only vestige of the traditional "Culture of Land" in the context of the socialist land property rights pattern in China.

I believe this was one of the fundamental reasons for skyrocketing housing expansion. Aside from the prohibition of private property in China, the financial repression (FR) policy discussed in the previous chapter also explains this policy. People had few options to invest in. Hence, real estate was considered a hedge of risks in crisis situations, and a guarantee of value under inflation.

The "Culture of Land" was important. However, China's economic environment, especially economic growth, was also indispensable.

2) Economic Growth

Economic growth was the first step for China to launch the housing reform and the basis for the Chinese government to terminate the welfare-based housing distribution system in 1998. With the increase in income, and especially disposable income of urban residents in China, the development of real estate became a feasible scenario in China.

Figure 20: Gross Domestic Product Growth of China, 1979-2009 in %

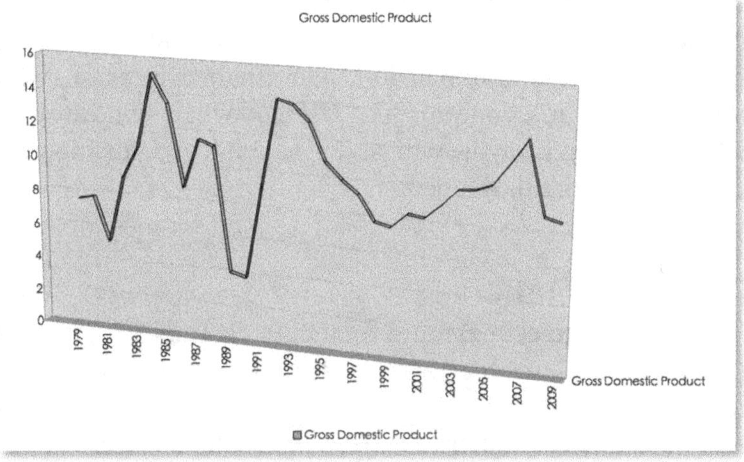

Source: Data 1990-2008 from China Statistical Yearbook 2009, 1979-1989 and 2009 from other sources of the NBSC

Figure 20 shows the evolution of GDP growth from 1979 to 2009. The average GDP growth during these last 31 years was 9.8%, or a growth of slightly less than 10%. But we cannot say that it was not a miracle.

If we only focus on the last 20 years from 1990 to 2009 (see the following figure), the average rate will be even higher. Of course, GDP cannot explain everything. In this paper, I consider the attitude of the Chinese government vis-à-vis GDP growth "Worship of GDP Growth". This "worship" can also lead to some negative consequences. We will discuss them further in the section on policy dilemmas. However, it is still one of the essential variables to evaluate a country's economic growth. For decision makers, GDP can also ensure social stability and social harmony in China - a country still with numerous heterogeneities and regional differences in terms of development level, natural conditions, religions and ethnicities.

In addition to culture and the economy, finance also plays an important role in the various determinants of China's real estate expansion, and finance is even more important in an economy like China, which continues to adopt FR. Savings growth and financial growth are two essential factors in finance.

2. Savings Growth

A lack of investment and financing channels in China is a thorny problem due to the FR, and though it has been loosened considerably since 1978, and the stock market and other financial markets often fluctuate, a huge number of household savings has to find an outlet. The State Bond issued by the central government and other bonds by local governments are able to absorb only part of household savings. As such, buying houses is, naturally, their best option in China.

1) Income Growth

Figure 21 depicts the per capita annual disposable income of urban households in value and index from 1978 to 2008. The data we use here refers to the income in nominal terms. Dramatic progress has been made in terms of disposable income in China's urban areas since 1978 from 343.40 RMB to 15,780.80 RMB in 2008, around 46 times higher in 31 years. If we consider the index, it will be 815.7 for 2008 against 100 for 1978. (See Table 3: Per Capita Annual Income and Engel's Coefficient of Urban and Rural Households for details)

The economic growth has provided a solid foundation for the housing reform and for the development of the housing market. And as urban residents share the fruits of this economic growth (the problem of inequality and polarization of rich and poor is not discussed here for the time being), the housing market became feasible. In addition, real estate requires financial support similar to other emerging market economies or emerged developed states. We will look at the savings growth in China since 1978, especially after 1998.

Figure 21: Per Capita Annual Disposable Income of Urban Households 1978-2008

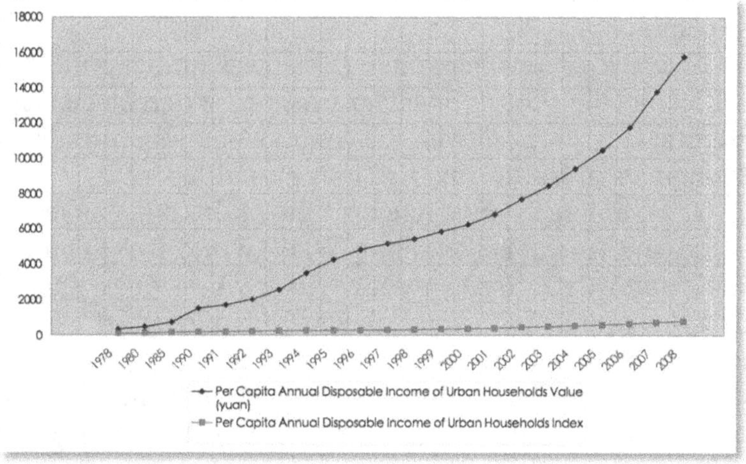

Source: China Statistical Yearbook 2009

As the GDP rose, so, too, did incomes, which led to bigger savings in China.

2) Savings Growth

We have already discussed multiple reasons why China enjoyed a high savings rate in Chapter 1.

Data from the Basic Conditions of Urban Households 2008 (NSBC, 2009) can complement the urban scenario: The national per capita annual income was 17,068 RMB in urban areas in 2008, and the per capita disposable income was 15,781 RMB against the per capita annual consumption expenditure of 11,243 RMB in 2008 in urban areas.

3) Savings for Housing

There were mixed feelings about the high savings rate of Chinese. This was a real dilemma not only for economists, but also for policy makers because too high a savings rate led to insufficient spending, and that this lack of consumption created an imbalance in the demand structure.

The lack of consumption in China was further criticized following the global financial crisis as external demand significantly dropped with the contraction of industrialized economies in North America, Europe and Japan.

The Chinese savings rate beat the peak savings rates of Japan and Korea, according to WDI (World Development Indicators) data. Japan reached its peak savings rate of 51.8% around 1970, and South Korea reached 50.7% around 2000, but they were all lower than the Chinese rate of 52% in 2008. If we compare China with India, Brazil and other middle-income countries with comparable economic growth levels, the Chinese savings rate is also much higher.

The Chinese savings rate was not only too high but continued its rapid ascent. The following figure shows the national savings rate and residents' savings rate (residents' savings / residents' disposable income) from 1992 and 2007 in China.

Figure 22: Evolution of Savings and Housing Prices in China from 1992 to 2007

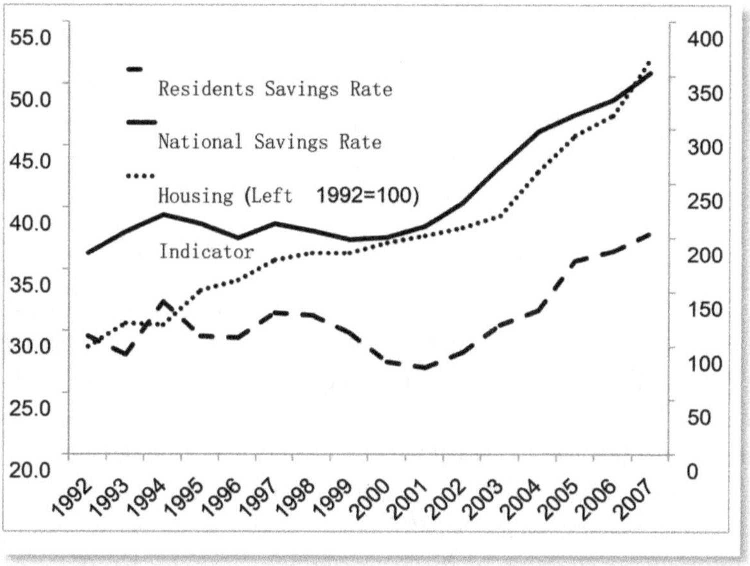

Source: China Statistical Yearbook 2009 and previous years

Figure 22 shows that the national savings rate had largely increased in China since 2000. The rate rose to 50.9% in 2007 from 37.6% in 2000. In the same period, residents' savings rate also grew from 27.5% to 37.5%.

The figure also shows changes in prices for commercialized residential housing from 1992 to 2007. After the stable rise from 1997 to 2003, housing prices in China rapidly increased starting 2004. The price for commercialized housing had increased from 2,359 RMB/M^2 in 2003 to 3,864 RMB/M^2 in 2007, or 63.8% higher than four years earlier or a 16% increase per year. Obviously, this is much higher than the growth of residents' income in the same period.

Figure 22 shows that with the rapid growth in savings, Chinese housing prices simultaneously increased even though savings were already high before the public housing system reform. Hence, my hypothesis is: The rise in housing prices will bring about the rise in the residents' total savings in China.

Chinese high savings is a hot theme, but isn't a new one. We will just mention the most recent literature on this. Chamon and Prasad (2010) discovered that housing can be one of the most influencing factors in the savings rate of urban residents. Unfortunately, they failed to pursue their research on the relationship between housing and residents' savings.

2011 is an especially important year for Chinese research in the relationship between savings and housing prices. We will mention four major contributions. WANG & WEN (2011) theoretically analyzed this relationship in arguing that the rise in housing prices will not necessarily influence the residents' savings rate because the buyer's negative savings can "neutralize" ("neutralization effect") the positive savings of households who prepare savings for buying homes. Nevertheless, their model is feasible mainly for SS (steady state) analysis. I do not share its feasibility for a transition economy like China's - a rapidly evolving economy. Hence, I take a skeptical view towards its "explainability" in the analysis of Chinese residents' savings behaviors.

Another researcher, KUANG (2011), studied the influence of housing prices on consumption based on city-level data. However, its micro-foundation is not so solid. WEI & ZHANG (2011) found that the gender imbalance can result in the rise of Chinese residents' savings and its influence on housing prices. However, they focused their attention on the influence of the gender imbalance without delving into the relationship between housing prices and residents' savings.

WANG & WEN (2011) successfully discovered that the housing reform and the rise in housing prices can probably bring about a rise in residents' savings rate, but failed to analyze the residents' savings behavior when expectations for housing price increases continue to exist. This scenario is the general situation since the start of the 21st century in China.

Finally, CHEN & YANG (2011) demonstrated that the 1998 housing reform forced more and more Chinese families to depend on their savings to buy real estate. This increased the urban residents' savings rate. As for the "neutralization effect" that we just mentioned, CHEN et al. (2010) studied the consumption and savings behavior of migrating groups, and discovered that the marginal consumption propensity of these groups is much lower than urban residents, while their savings rate is much higher than urban residents.

Therefore, it is necessary to deepen the study on the relationship between the residents' savings rate and housing prices in China.

3. Financial Growth

The financial repression policy adopted in China for more than half a century had to evolve due to the economic growth and the changes in income structure brought by the market-oriented economic reform. Together with or soon after the launch of the economic reform, it was the turn of financial growth. Though China is still often criticized as one of the examples of financial repression states in the world, and though it is true in my opinion that compared with its miraculous economic success and China's financial reform and growth still lagged behind, China's finance progressed rapidly.

1) Broad Money Supply (M2) Growth

Figure 23: Money Supply in China at Year-end 1978-2000 (in 100 millions of RMB)

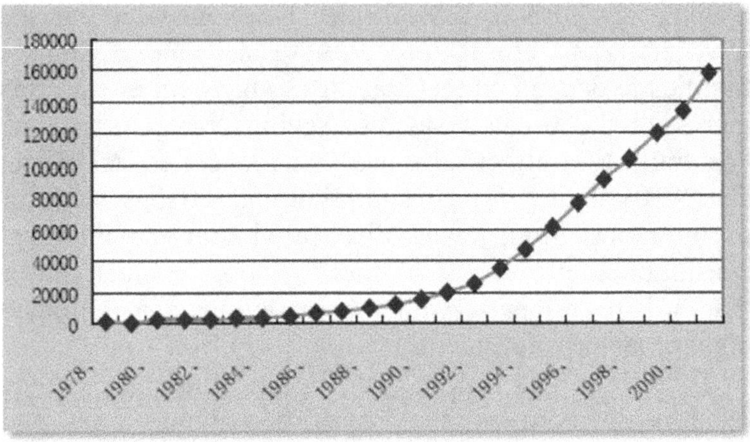

Source: National Bureau of Statistics of China

Figure 23 shows the growth of broad money (M2) in China since 1978 to 2000. In 1978, the M2 balance was near 150 billion RMB, but by the end of 2001, it reached slightly over 15,830 billion RMB, an increase of 106-fold over the first two decades of economic reform.

Since we will focus on the period from the start of the 1990s, refer to the following figure from 1990 to 2008. From 1,529 billion in 1990 to 47,517 billion RMB in 2008, the increase was 31-fold.

Figure 24: Money Supply in China at Year-end, 1990-2008 (in 100 million RMB)

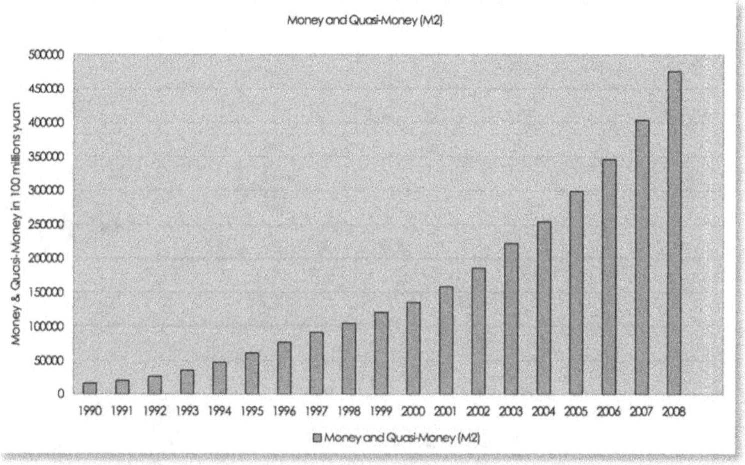

Source: China Statistical Yearbook 2009; Remarks: a) Since June in 2001, margin account of security companies maintained with financial institutions, part of Other Deposits, are included in M2.

2) Financial Interrelation Ratio (FIR) Growth

Figure 25 shows the Financial Interrelation Ratio (FIR) in China from 1978 to 2000. The FIR is the ratio of the total value of all financial assets to national wealth, which can be approximated by the GDP. Low FIR normally characterizes the early stages of financial development.

In this figure, the increase in FIR in China surprisingly rises from less than 40% to 165% in 2001. But this result is easy to understand because in the first stage of economic reform, monetization and national income were very low as previously discussed in this paper.

Figure 25: Financial Interrelation Ratio (FIR) in China at Year-end 1978-2000 (in %)

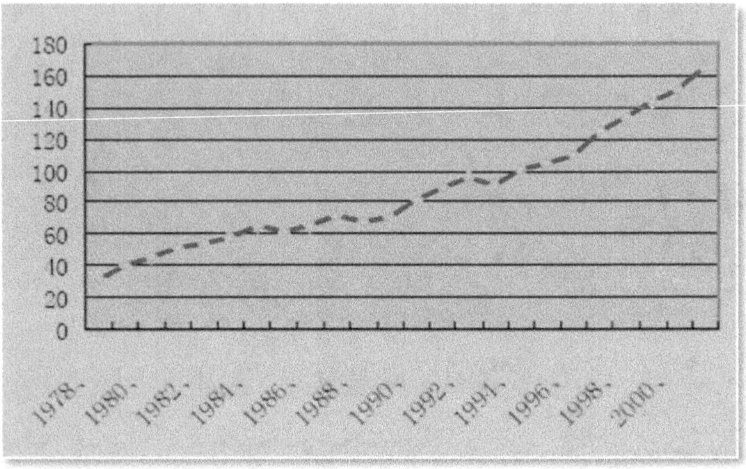

Source: National Bureau of Statistics of China

The factors which contributed to the increase in FIR are economic growth, institutional changes, financial deepening and the absence of credit.

♣ **Economic growth:**

The foundation of this progress was high economic growth and the change in the national income distribution pattern. We have just seen the dramatic progress in income. With economic progress, the structure of income distribution had also changed. In short, the government and enterprises saw their share in the national income drop while households saw their share rise as shown in Figure 21.

This change in the national income distribution pattern and the rise in household income paved the way for the foundation for the housing reform because the financial liberalization did not fundamentally begin in that period and the payments for the purchase of public housing before 1998 had to be generated only by household savings. We will only discuss the scenario until the end of the 20th century. For the scenario from the start of the 21st century, we will show later in this paper that the trend reversed after the end of the 20th century.

♣ **Institutional changes:**

China adopted the planned economy for half a century, and the economic reform since 1978 was meant to transform from a planned economy to a market economy. With the economic reform, the economic institutions and the political institutions had considerably evolved. The increasing decentralization of power gave the population greater freedom and more choices, but the institutional changes also brought higher uncertainty to the population who had to save more. The savings has naturally become a major tool against potential risks in case of the absence of a social security system in that period.

♣ **Financial deepening:**

The financial reform started after the economic one. One method of China's financial deepening was the monetization of economic activities because under the planned system, as shown in Figure 24, the need for broad money (M2) was only around 150 billion RMB in the first year of economic reform. It was higher in the country's monetization ratio, and its financial system was more developed.

♣ **Absence of Credit :**

Consumer credit was virtually non-existent in China before the economic reform and during the first phase of reform. The first consumer housing credit started only after the termination of the welfare-based housing distribution system. It was the 1998 "Resolutions" (Guofa 199823) that provided explicitly for the first time that all commercial banks would be able to grant personal housing loans in all urban areas.

The above four reasons made the FIR increase significantly from less than 40% in 1978 to 165% in 2001. A higher FIR represents a relatively mature stage of financial development, or, in short, a more developed financing sector with a high weight of this sector in the overall economy.

If I put the M2/GDP and FA/GDP (FA stands for financial assets in this book) together in Figure 26, the gap between these two variables is rather obvious. At the beginning of 1978, the blue line and the rose line overlapped. This was due to the unitary financial asset structure at the very first stage of economic reform in China, as China did not have other financial assets except deposits and cash. This corresponds to the fact that in 1979, deposits and cash represented 83.57% and 16.43%, respectively, of total financial assets. In other words, there were no other non-monetary financial assets at all, and the broad money balance was almost equal to the total value of financial assets.

With the development of economic reform, the rose line started to exceed the blue one, and a significant gap emerged around a decade after 1978. Look at the year 2000: The gap was rather large already. A great change in the financial pattern took place in China. The share of deposits and cash dropped to 73.85% and 10.79% (combined around 85%). The remainder would go to government bonds, stock and insurance at 8.92%, 4.28% and 1.24%, respectively.

The expansion of China's stock market offered an opportunity at first to a big number of savers in China, part of whom had become investors or speculators. As numerous fluctuations in the market gave these investors a strong sense of insecurity, the majority of these investors had to search for other channels for their savings to generate added value. The stock market expansion had offered an excellent chance for real estate developers to generate funds from the market.

Bonds were limited in quantity. They were less attractive for risk-takers due to the low returns and required long-term investments. Insurance was minuscule compared to the market and bonds. Hence, the partial negative effects of the market on individuals' savings were largely compensated by the positive effects of the financing of developers from the market to acquire complementary funds for their real estate projects, which usually lacked funds despite bank loans, down payments from housing purchasers (original savers) and their own capital.

Figure 26: Difference between M2/GDP and FA/GDP in China at Year-end, 1978-2000 (in %)

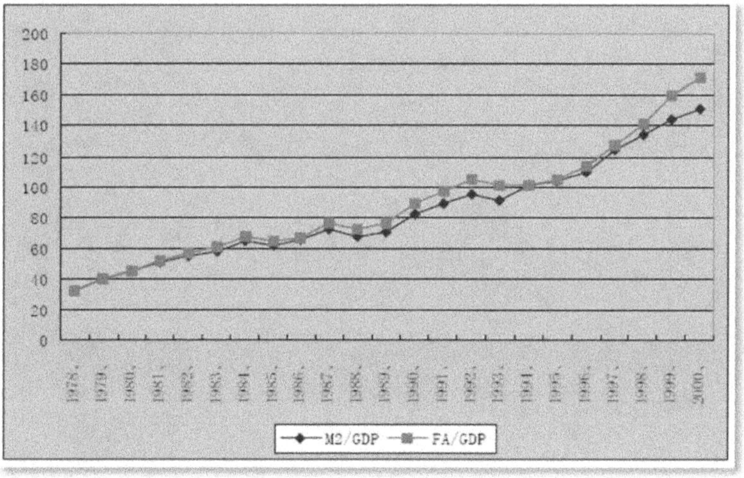

Source: National Bureau of Statistics of China

We have discussed multiple “fuels” for the housing market expansion: the “Culture of Land” was the cultural roots for Chinese people and the starting point of our discussion on the surge in housing prices. The GDP growth and the income growth represented an economic foundation which would pave the road for the housing reform and for the housing market development, while the savings growth directly provided the “fuel” for the housing “car” for households who wanted to buy properties. Finally, the financial growth provided the financial backbone, with more supply of M2 and the monetization of economic activities. Thus, the housing reform and real estate market started their phenomenal advance.

CONCLUSION

China's restructuring in finance i.e. in the banking and credit systems, especially its WTO-oriented reforms, have contributed to the stability of China's economic growth. As policy recommendations have been given to Chinese decision makers along with previous sections of this book, we will only review the following points:

On banking and credit reforms, the non-State-owned financial intermediaries remained a "decoration" in the country's financial system, and this will complicate the efficiency amelioration in the allocation of financial resources and investment in projects that are not State-owned but more innovative or profitable. Therefore, we should adopt in-depth or substantial restructuring in the banking and financial sectors.

The NPLs represent one of thorniest problems for Chinese authorities as almost all Chinese SOBs will go bankrupt if strict Western banking standards are adopted. We should applaud the huge efforts the Chinese government has made so far to peel NPLs, but a permanent solution is being sought to make these SOBs financially more independent and internationally more competitive.

Generally speaking, the restructuring of Chinese real estate has been a success. However almost all of the sector is still under the control of the State not only at the national level but also the local level. The market—this "invisible hand"—should play a more important role to maintain a healthy and harmonious development of the Chinese real estate sector.

On savings, this variable has contributed a lot to China's economic growth and the expansion of the real estate market over several decades. However, real estate has become a burden for Chinese residents, especially for younger generations, and this distortion has generated increasing socio-economic problems. Hence, new politics should be adopted so as to reduce the weight of real estate and to ensure a more rational and balanced consumption in Chinese society.

BIBLIOGRAPHY

The Law of Land Administration of the People's Republic of China: Different versions adopted on June 25, 1986, amended on December 29, 1988 and August 29, 1998;

Fan H. S., ed. 1999: Chinese Real Estate Market. Wuhan: Hubei People's Publishing House;

Tang G. 1989: "Urban Housing System Reform in China." Paper presented at the Joint Seminar of Housing System Reform in China, Beijing;

Wang Y. P. & A. Murie, 1996: "The Process of Commercialization of Urban Housing in China.";

Wang Y. P. & A. Murie, 2000: "Social and Spatial Implications of Housing Reform in China.";

Zhang X. Q. & Hong M. W., 1993 : The Sociology of Housing, Edition: Social Sciences Academic Press;

"Survey of Rent on 1783 Households", 1953, Beijing Real Estate Administration Bureau, and other statistics of this Bureau;

"Thinking about the Housing Reform Process in China" (Fu B., 1997);

"The Rent Standard for the Public Housing", amended in July 1952;

"Rent Standard for Public Housing for Civil Use", executed in 1958;

Tian J. G., 2010: "Remembrances of the Republic";

http://www.51Labour.com/ China Labour Consultation Website;

The “Dwelling Narrowness”, a super-hot TV series in 2009 in China,
Zhang H., 2009: “Housing reform by urban redevelopment in China”;
Chiu R. L. H., 1996: “Housing Affordability in Shenzhen Special Economic Zone: A Forerunner of China’s Housing Reform.” Housing Studies 11(4);
“Decision on the Deepening of Urban Housing System Reform” (Guofa 199443), promulgated by the State Council of P. R. C. in July 1994;
“The Resolutions on Continuing Urban Housing System Reform, Accelerating Housing Development” (Guofa 199823), promulgated by the State Council of P. R. C. In July 1998;
“The Several Opinions of the State Council on Solving the Housing Difficulties of Urban Low-Income Families” (No.24 [2007], promulgated by the State Council of P. R. C. In August 2007;
“Survey Report on China’s Urbanization Rate”, Versions 2008 & 2009, By China International Urbanization Development Strategy Research Commission;
Series of Reports on “New China’s 60 Years Achievements”, September 17 2009, By the National Bureau of Statistics of China;
The Bluebook, April 14th 2010, by Chinese Academy of Social Sciences,
Mr. WANG X. F. (2008), one of 10 experts of the Beijing Old City Protection Consultancy Group;
Mr. BAI J. Z. (2008), another member of this Group;
Lu G., 2010: “Achievements and Challenges: 30 Years of Housing Reforms in the People’s Republic of China”;
Wang Z. H., 2009, Senior Economist of the Chartered Bank: “Debate on China’s Urbanization Rate”;
Chen G. Q., Director of the Institute of Real Estate Studies, Peking University, Interview by “Securities Times” (*Zhengquan Shibao*) in April 2010;

Mr. Ba S. S. from the Development Research Center of the State Council (DRC),
2009 Statistical Communiqué of National Economic and Social Development;
Overview Statistical Communiqué of House in Urban Town of 2002, July 16th 2003 by the Ministry of Construction;
Overview Statistical Communiqué of House in Urban Town of 2005, July 4th 2006 by the Ministry of Construction;
Xie, Y. & H. Liu., 2004.: "Price-Rent Ratio in China's Housing Market: Proper Interval, Measurement and an Empirical Study.";
Ma Y. Q. E., 2005: "Housing Price Bubbles in 37 Major Cities.";
Hui E. C. M. & Y. Shen., 2006 : "Housing Price Bubbles in Hong Kong, Beijing and Shanghai: A Comparative Study." ;
"The Law of Land Administration of the People's Republic of China", adopted on June 25, 1986; amended on December 29, 1988 and August 29, 1998;
"Interim Regulations of the People's Republic of China Concerning the Assignment and Transfer of the Right to the Use of the State-owned Land in the Urban Areas" (May 19th 1990, State Council);
The Property Law of the People's Republic of China, approved by China's National Congress on 16th March 2007;
Speech by Mr. Zhou X. C. on February 10th 2010 in Malaysia.
Elisa OSSOLA, 2013: "An Econometric Analysis of Time-Varying Risk Premia in Large Cross-Sectional Equity Datasets";
Julio Escolano et al, "The Puzzle of Persistently Negative Interest Rate-Growth Differentials: Financial

Repression or Income Catch-up?", IMF Working Paper, WP/11/260, November 2011;
Shaw, Edward S. Financial Deepening in Economic Development. New York: Oxford University Press, 1973;
McKinnon, Ronald I. Money and Capital in Economic Development. Washington D.C.: Brookings Institute, 1973;
Ronald McKinnon, "Money and Capital in Economic Development", Brookings Institute, Washington D.C., 1973;
Reinhart, Carmen M. & Sbrancia, M. Belen, "The Liquidation of Government Debt", NBER working paper, 2011;
Reinhart, Carmen M. and Rogoff, Kenneth S., This Time is Different. Princeton and Oxford: Princeton University Press, 2008, p. 143;
Bill Gross, "The Caine Mutiny (Part 2)", May 03, 2011;
LIN Yifu et al., "Chinese Miracle: Development Strategy & Economic Reforms", First version, 1994;
Jean-Claude Maswana, "China's Financial Development and Economic Growth: Exploring the Contradictions", International Research Journal of Finance and Economics, Issue 19 (2008);
WANG Qinmin, President of All China Federation of Industry and Commerce, Speech, February 2nd 2013;
Government Revenue from Financial Repression Giovannini, Alberto and de Melo, Martha, The American Economic Review, Vol. 83, No. 4 Sep. 1993 (pp. 953-963);
Paul A. Samuelson, <An Exact Consumption-Loan Model of Interest with or without the Social Contrivance of Money>, Journal of Political Economy, Vol.66, No.6, P467-482, 1958;
Julio Escolano et al, "The Puzzle of Persistently Negative Interest Rate-Growth Differentials: Financial

Repression or Income Catch-up?", IMF Working Paper, WP/11/260, November 2011;
Chi Lo, "Chinese Interest Rates: From Financial Repression To Liberalization", January 2014;
Reinhart, Kirkegaard, Sbrancia, "Financial Repression Redux", IMF Finance and Development, June 2011, p. 22-26;
Anne-Laure Delatte, Julien Fouquau & Carsten A. Holz, "Explaining money demand in China during the transition from a centrally planned to a market-based monetary system", BOFIT Discussion Papers 27/2011, October 2011;
"2012: Market Investigation Report of Financial NPA Market in China", by China Orient Asset Management Co.;
"Interim Provisions on absorption of foreign capital financial Asset Management Co to participate in asset restructuring and disposal", 26 October 2001;
NPA investigation made by PricewaterhouseCoopers (PWC) in China on May 2005;
R. P. Pradhan, P. D. & S. Bele, "Financial Development And Economic Growth In BRICs: A Panel Data Analysis", Journal of Quantitative Economics, Vol. 11 Nos. 1 & 2 (Combined), January-July 2013;
K.C. Chen, L. Wu & J. Wen, "The relationship between finance and growth in China", Global Finance Journal 24 (2013) 1-12;
J. Zhang, L. Wang & S. Wang, "Financial development and economic growth: Recent evidence from China", Journal of Comparative Economics 40 (2012) 393-413;
Chao, C.C., Laffargue, J.P. and Yu, E. (2011) "The Chinese saving puzzle and the life-cycle hypothesis : A revaluation", China Economic Review, 22: 108-120;
Laffargue, J.P. and Yu, E. (2013a), "The Chinese savings puzzles";

Laffargue, J.P. and Yu, E. (2013b), "Consumption, investment and savings in China";
B. DING,, "Study on Marxism" 2, 29th August 2013;
G. LI, "Economic Management" 2, February 2007;
J. CHEN, "Sixty Years of Housing in China: Review and Reflexions", May 2012;
J. G. LI et al., "Collection of Papers on Reform", 2007;
"China Statistical Yearbook", 1992;
Chinese Academy of Social Sciences, "World Economic Handbook", Version 1981, P121;
"China Statistical Yearbook", 1983, P495.

TABLE OF CONTENTS

CHINE
AUX ÉDITIONS L'HARMATTAN

Dernières parutions

LE ZODIAQUE CHINOIS INSOLITE
Un ouvrage pour découvrir ce qui fait rire les Chinois ?
Véronique Michel
Le zodiaque chinois insolite est un outil linguistique original et indispensable pour apprendre en s'amusant : vocabulaire clé, adages et dictons sont ici abordés. À travers l'exemple des signes astrologiques, cet ouvrage permet aux lecteurs de s'initier à la sagesse traditionnelle, aux coutumes ainsi qu'à la culture d'hier et d'aujourd'hui de l'empire du Milieu. Loin des stéréotypes et des idées reçues, la culture populaire et l'humour donnent une vision décalée d'une société chinoise en perpétuelle mutation.
Sépia (190 p., 20 euros)
ISBN : 979-10-334-0148-3, EAN EBOOK : 9791033405092

PROVERBES CHINOIS ET STÉRÉOTYPES
Les animaux des 12 signes du zodiaque dans les proverbes chinois
Palizhati S. Yiltiz
Voici une invitation à découvrir l'univers et la tradition chinoises. Pour pénétrer dans cette culture, une des plus anciennes, nous utilisons la porte des proverbes, et plus particulièrement ceux qui sont liés aux animaux des 12 signes du zodiaque chinois.
(204 p., 20,5 euros)
ISBN : 978-2-343-16361-1, EAN EBOOK : 9782140117503

MON ÂME... TA PORTE RESTÉE ENTROUVERTE
Ruling ZHANG
Du pays aimant au pays aimé, sans cesse vont les pas et la voyageuse nous laisse apercevoir l'âme traversière qui l'habite et celle de ses deux patries, la Chine et la France. Elle nous révèle ses sentiments profonds avec pudeur et générosité mais surtout elle exprime avec humilité le recueillement extrême que la Nature lui inspire pour mieux appréhender le sens que doit revêtir pour elle la vie, une vie que les Hommes négligent souvent par inconscience ou par intérêt. Elle entrouvre une porte au lecteur sur les origines d'une histoire particulière autant qu'universelle. On reconnaîtra aisément certaines grandes influences philosophiques, littéraires de Chine. À travers ce recueil en version bilingue, elle enrichit la poésie chinoise contemporaine non moins que le langage poétique universel.
(Coll. Poètes des cinq continents, 144 p., 15 euros)
ISBN : 978-2-343-17156-2, EAN EBOOK : 9782140117060

UNION EUROPÉENNE AFRIQUE-CHINE

Jeu et enjeux pour la paix

Séraphin Moundounga

Préface d'Emmanuel Caulier

Pendant que l'UE, pour sa sécurité et sa stabilité, ainsi que pour la paix en Afrique et le développement de ce continent, oeuvre à promouvoir les Droits de l'Homme, la Chine a proposé et obtenu de l'Afrique la signature d'un partenariat alternatif condamnant toute coopération économique conditionnant l'aide au développement à la promotion des Droits de l'Homme. Ce partenariat est de nature à compromettre l'amélioration de la gouvernance africaine. L'appropriation des valeurs démocratiques par l'Union africaine est-elle capitalisable pour une démocratisation africaine garante du développement inclusif, pour la paix durable en Afrique, la stabilité et la prospérité en Europe ? C'est à ces questions du triangle Europe-Afrique-Chine que répond cet ouvrage destiné aux acteurs politiques et diplomates, aux opérateurs économiques, aux chercheurs et étudiants.

(Coll. Diplomatie et stratégie, 516 p., 42 euros)

ISBN : 978-2-343-16590-5, EAN EBOOK : 9782140115721

PARLONS BALTI

Au pays du K2 - Pakistan

Karim Khan Saka

Préface de Brigitte et Michel Grelaud

La langue balti est considérée comme l'ancienne forme de la langue tibétaine. Selon un sondage, le balti est parlé aujourd'hui par 770 000 personnes. En dehors du Tibet, on l'emploie dans trois provinces de la Chine (Xinjiang, Sichuan et Yunnan), au Bhoutan, au Népal et en Inde (Sikkim, Poraig, Ladakh). Au Baltistan, dans le nord du Pakistan, cette langue est parlée par une population de 400 000 personnes.

(Coll. Parlons, 166 p., 18 euros)

ISBN : 978-2-343-16962-0, EAN EBOOK : 9782140114960

LA CHINE, MIROIR DE NOS PASSIONS

Radiographie de la sinophilie et de la sinophobie

Claude Geoffroy

L'Europe, en particulier la France, a de tout temps entretenu avec la Chine une relation passionnelle alternant des moments d'engouements et des accès d'hostilité. Au gré d'une confrontation des écrits produits sur la Chine à diverses époques (Lettres des jésuites arrivés en Chine au XVIIe siècle, articles des philosophes des Lumières, littérature maoïste, ouvrages représentatifs actuels) se dessinent certaines inclinations, tantôt révélatrices des passions d'une époque, tantôt symptomatiques de penchants plus profonds.

(Coll. Questions contemporaines, 150 p., 16,5 euros)

ISBN : 978-2-343-16674-2, EAN EBOOK : 9782140111662

LA DIPLOMATIE COMMERCIALE DE LA CHINE

Ming Fei Gu

La diplomatie commerciale de la Chine résulte d'un processus complexe. Depuis son accession à l'OMC en 2001, la Chine a affirmé à plusieurs reprises sa confiance et son optimisme pour le système commercial multilatéral. Or, comme tous les grands pays, sa diplomatie commerciale ne se limite pas au multilatéralisme, elle comporte aussi une très forte propension vis-à-vis du régionalisme et du bilatéralisme. Plus récemment, le projet dit des « Nouvelles Routes de la Soie » lancé en automne 2013, est devenu la stratégie centrale de la diplomatie commerciale chinoise à l'ère de Xi Jinping, qui a pour objectif de promouvoir la coopération régionale, et de renforcer l'influence économique et politique de la Chine dans les pays riverains.

(Coll. Développement et Mondialisation, 194 p., 20 euros)

ISBN : 978-2-343-16192-1, EAN EBOOK : 9782140109799

PREMIÈRES LECTURES EN CHINOIS

Volume 1

Un livre de lecture bilingue chinois-français pour enfants

Marijana Benesh Weiner, Dominique Groux, Wu Yuying

Illustrations de Getachew Bernahu

Ce livre, constitué de deux volumes, est destiné aux enfants qui commencent l'apprentissage du chinois à l'école ou à la maison. Ils y découvriront vingt histoires en chinois, avec des traductions en français auxquelles ils peuvent se référer. La difficulté des textes est progressive, ce sont les tournures syntaxiques de base et les temps les plus courants des verbes qui sont utilisés ici. Les enfants prennent ainsi l'habitude de lire des textes relativement longs en chinois et sans se décourager.

(74 p., 15 euros)

ISBN : 978-2-343-15785-6, EAN EBOOK : 9782140105265

LA DIPLOMATIE CULTURELLE DE LA RÉPUBLIQUE POPULAIRE DE CHINE

Enjeux et limites d'une "offensive de charme"

Audrey Bonne

Depuis le début des années 1980, la République populaire de Chine opère une ouverture sur le monde et cette ouverture s'accompagne d'une volonté de rayonnement culturel. Riche d'une histoire plurimillénaire, la Chine promeut activement la diffusion de la culture chinoise sur la scène internationale. À l'ère de la mondialisation, cet ouvrage esquisse une analyse des implications, des réussites en termes de soft power et des échecs de la diplomatie culturelle menée par le gouvernement chinois depuis 2002.

(Coll. Points sur l'Asie, 244 p., 24,5 euros)

ISBN : 978-2-343-16149-5, EAN EBOOK : 9782140106538

LA PENSÉE MUSICALE DE JEAN-JACQUES ROUSSEAU EN CHINE

Na Zhang

Préface de Violaine Anger

En Chine, la notation musicale dite jianpu (notation simplifiée) qui représente les sons musicaux par des chiffres indo-arabes est la plus utilisée, mais elle n'est pas chinoise à l'origine : elle vient d'Occident et plus précisément d'une pensée développée par Jean-Jacques Rousseau en 1742 qui n'a pas connu le succès à l'époque en Europe. L'ouvrage analyse cette méthode astucieuse et ce phénomène de sinisation.

(Coll. L'univers esthétique, 298 p., 31 euros)

ISBN : 978-2-343-15786-3, EAN EBOOK : 9782140105852

POLITIQUE LINGUISTIQUE INTÉRIEURE DE LA CHINE : ENTRE UNITÉ ET DIVERSITÉ

Le débat autour du cantonais au début du XXIe siècle

Préface de Joël Bellassen

Yufei Guo

Des années 1950 à nos jours, la priorité de la politique linguistique chinoise est accordée à la standardisation et à la promotion du mandarin. Or, durant l'été 2010, à Guangzhou (Canton) et à Hong Kong, des manifestations pour la défense du cantonais et leur retombées médiatiques ont contribué à révéler un sujet longtemps mis à l'écart dans la politique du gouvernement de la Chine : celui des "dialectes", que le présent ouvrage n'hésite pas à aborder.

(Coll. Espaces discursifs, 326 p., 35 euros)

ISBN : 978-2-343-15093-2, EAN EBOOK : 9782140102721

EVOLUTION D'UNE VILLE CHINOISE

La mutation de Wuhan à l'époque moderne (1861-1949)

Jun Li

Préface de Pierre Clément

Dans la dynamique des villes chinoises, la confrontation entre tradition orientale et influence occidentale a marqué un tournant. L'évolution urbaine dans cette période est particulièrement significative pour la ville de Wuhan, située au coeur du territoire chinois et qui, bien qu'éloignée de la côte, a connu l'implantation d'une série de concessions étrangères, mais aussi un développement proprement chinois parallèle. Abondamment illustré, l'ouvrage présente les circonstances et les résultats de cette mutation, tant en termes d'architecture pour diverses fonctions, que d'organisation urbaine et de centralité.

(264 p., 30 euros)

ISBN : 978-2-343-15853-2, EAN EBOOK : 9782140103049

Structures éditoriales du groupe L'Harmattan

L'Harmattan Italie
Via degli Artisti, 15
10124 Torino
harmattan.italia@gmail.com

L'Harmattan Hongrie
Kossuth l. u. 14-16.
1053 Budapest
harmattan@harmattan.hu

L'Harmattan Sénégal
10 VDN en face Mermoz
BP 45034 Dakar-Fann
senharmattan@gmail.com

L'Harmattan Cameroun
TSINGA/FECAFOOT
BP 11486 Yaoundé
inkoukam@gmail.com

L'Harmattan Burkina Faso
Achille Somé – tengnule@hotmail.fr

L'Harmattan Guinée
Almamya, rue KA 028 OKB Agency
BP 3470 Conakry
harmattanguinee@yahoo.fr

L'Harmattan RDC
185, avenue Nyangwe
Commune de Lingwala – Kinshasa
matangilamusadila@yahoo.fr

L'Harmattan Congo
67, boulevard Denis-Sassou-N'Guesso
BP 2874 Brazzaville
harmattan.congo@yahoo.fr

L'Harmattan Mali
Sirakoro-Meguetana V31
Bamako
syllaka@yahoo.fr

L'Harmattan Togo
Djidjole – Lomé
Maison Amela
face EPP BATOME
ddamela@aol.com

L'Harmattan Côte d'Ivoire
Résidence Karl – Cité des Arts
Abidjan-Cocody
03 BP 1588 Abidjan
espace_harmattan.ci@hotmail.fr

L'Harmattan Algérie
22, rue Moulay-Mohamed
31000 Oran
info2@harmattan-algerie.com

L'Harmattan Maroc
5, rue Ferrane-Kouicha, Talaâ-Elkbira
Chrableyine, Fès-Médine
30000 Fès
harmattan.maroc@gmail.com

Nos librairies en France

Librairie internationale
16, rue des Écoles – 75005 Paris
librairie.internationale@harmattan.fr
01 40 46 79 11
www.librairieharmattan.com

Librairie l'Espace Harmattan
21 bis, rue des Écoles – 75005 Paris
librairie.espace@harmattan.fr
01 43 29 49 42

Lib. sciences humaines & histoire
21, rue des Écoles – 75005 Paris
librairie.sh@harmattan.fr
01 46 34 13 71
www.librairieharmattansh.com

Lib. Méditerranée & Moyen-Orient
7, rue des Carmes – 75005 Paris
librairie.mediterranee@harmattan.fr
01 43 29 71 15

Librairie Le Lucernaire
53, rue Notre-Dame-des-Champs – 75006 Paris
librairie@lucernaire.fr
01 42 22 67 13

www.ingramcontent.com/pod-product-compliance
Lightning Source LLC
LaVergne TN
LVHW021232061026
849535LV00008B/3021